Organize

A Week-by-week Guide to Simplify Your Space

(Effective Strategies to Make Time for What Matters Most to You)

Frank Ferrell

Published By **Elena Holly**

Frank Ferrell

All Rights Reserved

Organize: A Week-by-week Guide to Simplify Your Space (Effective Strategies to Make Time for What Matters Most to You)

ISBN 978-1-77485-650-5

No part of this guidebook shall be reproduced in any form without permission in writing from the publisher except in the case of brief quotations embodied in critical articles or reviews.

Legal & Disclaimer

The information contained in this ebook is not designed to replace or take the place of any form of medicine or professional medical advice. The information in this ebook has been provided for educational & entertainment purposes only.

The information contained in this book has been compiled from sources deemed reliable, and it is accurate to the best of the Author's knowledge; however, the Author cannot guarantee its accuracy and validity and cannot be held liable for any errors or omissions. Changes are periodically made to this book. You must consult your doctor or get professional medical advice before using any of the suggested remedies, techniques, or information in this book.

Upon using the information contained in this book, you agree to hold harmless the Author from and against any damages, costs, and expenses, including any legal fees potentially resulting from the application of any of the information provided by this guide. This disclaimer applies to any damages or injury caused by the use and application, whether directly or indirectly, of any advice or information presented, whether for breach of contract, tort, negligence, personal injury, criminal intent, or under any other cause of action.

You agree to accept all risks of using the information presented inside this book. You need to consult a professional medical practitioner in order to ensure you are both able and healthy enough to participate in this program.

TABLE OF CONTENTS

Introduction 1

Chapter 1: Organization Secrets That Will Make Your Work Life Easy 7

Chapter 2: What To Do? Create An Organizational System That Is Suitable For You 23

Chapter 3: How To Organize Your Work Space To Boost Productivity 40

Chapter 4: Fast And Easy Way To Handle Hard Copies 56

Chapter 5: How To Manage Your Time To Do More With Less Stress 72

Chapter 6: Digital Organization Strategies For Rapid Access To Information 88

Chapter 7: Easy Ways To Stay Current In Important Business Communication 105

Chapter 8: Tips To Make Your System Flexible To Career Advancement 118

Chapter 9: Organizing Your Basement, Storage Spaces And Attics 131

Chapter 10: Maintaining Your Organization
.... 136
Chapter 11: General Tips 141
Conclusion 184

Introduction

A lot of people believe that they're held back by they don't have the organizational skills. Being organized and well-organized is vital to maximize efficiency and achieve your potential to the fullest, but even if you've been criticized for being unorganized or don't have an organization system that you like does not mean that you aren't organized. Actually, you probably have an organized system, but that method isn't efficient. The majority of us have our system of organization within our heads and it can be effective for a time, but eventually our brains get overwhelmed and we lose data. It is difficult to remember the place you placed the important document. It is difficult to remember which tasks you must work on. You miss important phone calls or meetings. You feel overwhelmed, and you realize that you must make changes but don't feel capable of doing the job.

So, put all your negative thoughts and thoughts out of the window since you can be organized. Take a look around your kitchen space for a second and you'll see a perfect example of your ability to organize. The plates are in one spot while the pans and pots in another, and the glasses are placed in their respective spaces, and food items too. It's not the most efficient way to organize your kitchen or you could be an irritant with dishes that are dirty or empty pizza box strewn across your counters but at certain levels, you know the place where everything has to be. Even if you weren't able to create the system your self, maybe a spouse, partner perhaps even parents arranged your kitchen. However, you've managed to manage your space in a certain degree. A kitchen is an excellent illustration of how to organize. When you enter the kitchen of a friend to grab some water You might have difficulty because they do not organize their home as yours, or in the manner you would manage your kitchen, if it were your choice. It's because everybody is organized differently, and the ultimate goal is an art of creating an organization that is beneficial to you. I'll teach you how to accomplish this.

If we're talking about the workplace or at home or your hobby, business or home or even your financial situation it is possible how to organize yourself. It's about taking the basic principles of organization using them to create systems that are clear to you. Even if you're in an organization of another it is possible to organize your tasks and items that you're accountable for in a manner that is logical to you and is compatible with the overall system.

For many it can feel like being organized is stifling and it's because they are still trying to keep track of things in their minds. They can generally provide you with the location of important information or information they require is at any time. The idea of having an exact location to store every item, and then making sure that you return them after they're finished seems like more work. However, the benefit of having organizing systems is that it lets you free your brain. If every item is in an appropriate place, you don't need to use your brain to keep track of all the projects, resources and files. It is possible to concentrate on work, creating, on being totally engaged with the work that is in front of you. A well-organized system can allow you to be at peace in your mind since you don't need to be concerned about not being able to attend appointments, forgetting things or losing crucial details. The system takes over the stress of all of those things so you can rest and focus on giving each task your best effort and each relationship with your full focus.

It's not easy to attain also. It is possible that you have tried methods of organization that did not fit your needs and you feel you're "unorganized." But the truth is that you've just not found the right system to match your talents. It's like an instruction manual, however when it's written using a language that is different from yours, or is it using an entirely different measurement system than the one you are using, it will not be a good fit for your needs. It might be designed to assist, but it results in frustration and can make your job harder. When you find an approach that matches the strengths you have, it can improve your productivity without making you mad. You could discover yourself in love with organization, because it's the first time, it is now clear to you.

You can organize yourself. I'll repeat it again you can organize yourself. Even if you've not had a problem with organization in any job or in your entire life, you are able to learn how to become organized. I'll demonstrate how. We'll look at the subject from all angles starting with a thorough understanding of what it is and what it's not. We'll look at the various types of organizational systems to ensure that we discover one that is suited to your strengths. We'll examine specific ways of organizing your space. We'll follow up with tips on how to manage the documents you have, how to manage your time and digital media so that everything functions together to help you become more efficient. We'll also look at how organizing improves communication. Finally, we'll discover how to adjust to the changing times to ensure you're well-organized as you advance within your field. Everything is at your fingertips So, why are you putting off? A life that's healthy and well-organized can be yours. Let's get started!

Chapter 1: Organization Secrets That Will Make Your Work Life Easy

It's not just about being obsessed with neatness, nor is it a complicated system to make life difficult. The organization should make your life more efficient. It should make your work easier to enable you to complete more tasks without putting in as much effort. It will increase your efficiency and improve your attitude towards your tasks that you need to perform every day. The system should be easy intuitive, and makes perfect sense to those who use it.

The majority individuals have some moment or another, been forced to a terribly complicated system that leave an unpleasant smell in the mouths of our friends. If the system you're using isn't a good fit for your abilities and personal preferences, it can be overwhelming however the solution isn't just to eliminate the system completely. Instead, you should discover a method of staying organized in a way that is appropriate for your needs. The concept of organization isn't a single size for all solution however, it is an individual method of integrating all the important information that you must keep track with.

A well-organized system of organization must keep track of your work as well as your resource allocation, the schedule, and your correspondence. Each aspect of your organization system must function like an efficient racing engine that pushes you towards your objectives. Imagine it this way that if you were racing taking part in a race over a long distance you'd require plenty of items. An emergency kit as well as water, food, or maybe some kind of shelter in the event that you are caught during the downpour. It is possible to attempt to complete your race carrying all of those things in your arms however, each time you required an item, you'd have to stop, put the entire thing down and find the thing you require, before taking it back and putting it back up. In contrast it would be nice to have a well-organized backpack organized with all the items you would require for the race, you'd benefit greatly. The organization system you use in the workplace is your bag. It should be set up in a way that each item is in a location in which it is secure and easily accessible. It should be possible to locate what you require quickly without having to go through the other stuff and breaking other items within the pack. The straps must be adjusted to ensure that it will fit you well, but not too heavy , and in no way too big. You must be able to effortlessly keep track of everything in your bag such as people, tasks and information as well as time.

It's not in a marathon However, you're navigating the often difficult waters of the job market. It is more than keep pace with other runners; you must beat the rest if you want to stay ahead and gain confidence in the safety of your work. Being organized is a fantastic way to make yourself more over your colleagues. It can make your day-to-day work more efficient and lessen the stress that you deal with.

You might be wondering whether organization is really that great and everybody is organized, then why can't everyone be organized? It's a great question, and the answer lies in two ways. Most people don't have the ability to be organized because the way they're taught how to be organized. Their parents were not well-organized, their manager isn't organized , and they've never had the opportunity to learn how to become organized. They simply muddle their way through everyday tasks, and juggling every task they have to cope with. They're tired, angry, and most likely exhausted. Another reason that people fail to organize is that it requires a bit of effort in the beginning. It would be wonderful that organization was an easy solution that didn't cost an ounce However, if you need to find an organization method that can make an enormous difference in your life at work you'll need find a method that is compatible, then think about all aspects of that method and then implement it. The best part is that once you've accomplished this, you'll be able to go downhill from there.

Imagine if you could dedicate just one day to focus on your organization and the results could accelerate your career in rockets. This is what having a system in place at work can do however that single day of work is sufficient to leave most people running around in chaos with their careers stagnant and their levels of stress in the red zone. If you are able to set aside some time in the beginning to organize your work, it can save you numerous hours in the future and make your day much more enjoyable. Let's take a look at all the elements of a successful organizing method.

A Place for Everything

Being able to keep track with your information is probably the primary aspect that organizing is a must. We all want to to find the documents we require quickly and efficiently but, the reality is that we aren't able to do this. Even if you've got only a tiny workspace, many people have stacks of papers, piles documents and notes written on paper scraps as well as empty envelopes. In the event that you've got drawers, they are likely stuffed with papers that you do not need and can't locate them if you really needed they.

Many people imagine organization as a garage in which every instrument is placed on a wall of pegboards with a color-coded outline on the back of each device to indicate the exact contents of every space. Imagine being disciplined for not putting files in the right location. This is an extreme example of organization however, the purpose for organization should be to help make life easier, not complicated. A system that is effective is than a computer, in which data is filed automatically according to alphabetical order. You might have folders inside folders, but you are aware of the exact location of files when you require them. Also, if information is stored in the wrong location, it may take a considerable amount of time to find it. It is essential to establish an organization method to manage your time that allows you to get your work done and if the system makes the most sense for you, then there will not be any problems the implementation.

A place for each item of information is similar to taking your desk off. If you have piles of documents and folders strewn across your desk, you become overwhelmed. It is difficult to keep track of important information and juggling deadlines. The mess can be a hassle and prevents you from working at your best. If each file is stored in a specific place and is accessible, you'll be able to rest assured that your files are secure and readily accessible. Additionally, a clean space allows you to put in the effort. It allows you to focus on the task in hand instead of getting bogged down by clutter or stressing about how to keep up with your work resources.

If you've never had the opportunity to organize your workspace , you can begin by identifying the things you most frequently use and then deciding on a location for it that is simple to reach whenever you require it. Also, identify the items which you will only use often and make a designated space for them that is available but not necessarily in reach. It may sound easy and it is. Most people do not even think about it. They pack files as much as they can and put unnecessary items on their workstations or desktops to help them better keep track of everything However, they're making their work even more challenging.

Locating Items Fast

Each item is assigned an area, you'll be able to locate it quickly. It's like organizing the luggage. If you're living in luggage for couple of days, you do not want your clothes, which you're planning to wear for the first day to be placed in the bottom of your suitcase. Instead, put your clothes on top and then put the clothes you'll need for the following day below that , and then on. This way, the clothing you require is simple to locate and simple to access.

The process of organizing your books doesn't have to be complicated; the purpose is to make your things easier. It isn't necessary to use your Dewey Decimal system to arrange your books. Instead, you can sort them by the subject or frequency of usage. It's not very practical to store files you aren't working on that you're working on, in the hall, in an office filing space. You'll waste your time rushing between your workstation to the filing room. You should instead designate the space on or inside your workstation for keeping open files. It isn't logical to keep old files on your workstation. If you've not used the file in the past, make sure you have a space for it so you don't have to think about it, and it doesn't be a nuisance to your workspace.

The majority of carpenters are aware of this. They might have a large collection of instruments, yet they just carry the tools they are likely to utilize on the job location. In addition they just put those they use the often in their belts. They may use their hammer several times during the day, and the cordless drill just once. It's not sensible to burden them with equipment they will not use frequently. Also, it isn't logical to move between their work area and their toolbox each time they have to hit a nail. Therefore, they have specific tools on their belts in order to be able to locate it anytime they need it. They also keep a few items in their vehicles to ensure they have them in case they require them. The remaining instruments at home till they find work where the tools are required.

Finding things quickly can make your life more enjoyable. You won't have to worry about trying to keep track of all the thoughts in your head. There won't be a need to look through drawers, stacks, and cabinetry every time you require an item. As you maintain your kitchen's organization and you know precisely where to locate plates, you can arrange your workspace to ensure that you can quickly find the information you need. It will also make you appear more professional when your superior requires details from you. A worker who is able to find the information they require quickly and efficiently creates an impression of success. There's no reason not to show those with an influence over your career with the impression that your work is reliable and well-organized.

An Organization that works for You

Being organized should not be an obstacle. It is supposed to fit like a glove. It should be logical to you. It should seem easy, almost like second-nature. When you have found an organizational structure that is right for your needs, it's simple to implement and appear sensible. It's not about being rigid or following the guidelines. It should be easy and efficient to allow you to accomplish more tasks.

Each of us has our own naturally gifted talents that we can use to develop our preferences, talents, and distinctive ways of working. In this guide, we'll label these qualities your strengths. Most people struggle in opposition to their strength. They believe that they need to take advantage of their weaknesses but forget about the assets that will really aid them in their professional and personal lives. It is essential to acknowledge your strengths. The traits that make you special are the ones that will make you valuable to your family, company and acquaintances. Your system of organization should be in line with your strengths. If you're a person who is best at working for lengthy periods of unbroken concentration, then you'll need an organization system that stores all the items you may require in your reach. If, on the other hand you prefer working in shorter bursts, it may be best to store the things you require in different locations. If you're feeling a bit cramped with the amount of work on your desk, then you'll require a system to allow you to store items. In contrast, if you prefer keeping the files you work on where you can easily access them You could create a system that lets your most recent projects are kept at your desk.

There's no right or wrong organization system, however many may be unsuitable for your needs. The goal is to find the one that is right for you, and then implement with that system. The effectiveness of organization is as much as you can make it. You can, for instance, have an excellent program, yet if don't use it, you'll end up in the same situation. However when your system isn't user-friendly or requires too long to complete and you're not any better in the long run. The aim is to discover the most efficient way to manage all the resources that are involved in your job to ensure that you have the best time hours working and achieve more than prior to the organization system being established.

People, Tasks information & Time

Your organizational system should create an area for each product you use. It should make things easy to locate, and allow you to get what you require quickly. The system you choose should be suited to your needs best, your strengths, and work style. The main objective of your organization system is to manage your work-related tasks and the people you're working with, and the data that is crucial to your work and to optimize your time. We'll go over each of these aspects more in the chapters to follow However, if the system isn't organized to manage your Tasks and People, Information & Time, it's not really working.

It's not uncommon to come across an application that is effective in a couple of areas. For instance , you may find the program that allows you to organize your correspondence and information however if it doesn't connect the information to specific tasks or save time, it's not an efficient system. It is possible that certain methods work while others don't such as, for instance, you might prefer the information portion of one application and time management part of another. It's okay, you're able to select and decide to build an individual system that you want however the most important thing is: do they fit? A well-organized system integrates your People, Tasks and Information & Time and connects them together so that when you make changes in one area that is part of your system it's visible in the other parts. For instance, if , for example, you must schedule changes to your meeting the system should remind you to communicate with all People involved , and reorganize your tasks daily so that you do not waste Time.

The good thing is that we are living in the digital age of computers and artificial assistants that can connect all your data in order to ensure you are at the top of your game. It's not necessary to have an organized flip chart that is color coded or carry around a heavy Day Planner to manage each task. There are applications and programs which connect your phone to your tablet or desktop computer. Cloud storage lets you access your data wherever there's access to an Internet connection. The process of organizing is easier than ever before. All you need is some knowledge. Let's take a look at what takes to develop an organization system that is right for your needs to make the most of your day-to-day work and your professional life.

Chapter 2: What To Do? Create An Organizational System That Is Suitable For You

There are many different organizational systems. Because each person is different We can all design systems that enable us to achieve our maximum performance without any two systems being identical. What is effective for one person isn't going to work for other person, or even for someone who does similar work using the same resources. The objective is to learn the best designs and implement them in the demands of your work in a manner that matches your personal style and abilities.

Each organizational structure differs, most are based on the four main motivators. The first is the culture of your workplace. If for instance, a characteristic of the organization that you are working for is the spontaneity of its employees or a refusal to adhere to a strict corporate structures, you may prefer to create a flexible and natural system. Labelling every item could be seen as being too rigid, so instead you can employ indicators that blend in with your surroundings to organize your calendar, documents, and other communications. e.g. a color coding system

Another aspect that many prefer to structure their lives around is their routine. This can be your energy level for the day or the timetable of your day. If, for instance, you are a frequent traveler in your daily life, you might not have much "office" time, and you may require as much work accomplished while on the move as you can. In that scenario, you may develop a portable system that relies on your tablet or smartphone in addition to the desktop PC. You could keep your schedule and running lists of tasks to complete a business software that allows you to manage your schedule and automate changes.

Your resources are an additional aspect of design. A lot of people create their organizational system to meet the demands of the objects they must keep up with. For example, if you work in an industry that has an abundance of documents that have to be passed across departments, then you may develop your system to assist you in keeping the records so it is easy to find the information you require and ensure that the task you're accountable for is passed on to the correct individuals at the appropriate moment. It is the same for those who must manage large amounts of inventory, and the human capital. You might not quit your workstation or your desk in a normal working day. However, if are accountable for a number of tasks, your organization system will allow you to manage everything.

In the end, there are those who are focused on achieving goals. They arrange their work and the manner in which they conduct themselves, to advance their careers, or to accomplish a particular target. You could, for instance, develop a system to help you to monitor the organization's goals or lets you be prepared to accept new tasks with little notice. This kind of system works great for individuals working who work in fast-paced environment where agility and achievements are vital.

One thing every organizational system has in common is they're "systems" or an organized method to organize work. Let's examine what exactly an organizational system is and then dig into organizational theories before laying out the tasks that can assist you in creating an organization system that will work for you.

Understanding Systems

In its simplest terms it is a set of actions comprised of a variety of individuals who work in order to achieve an desired outcome. Imagine it as an old-fashioned clock. There are many, sometimes hundreds of parts that make up a clock, all doing specific tasks that are all contributing to the objective of keeping track of time. Your system of organization is similar. There are two major reasons for why an organization system may not be effective. The first is that the system needs to contain the appropriate actions. For example, if you are a manager who is in charge of scheduling large numbers of workers, you must perform a few important tasks you need to perform before you actually make the schedule. It is essential to understand what roles are required in all times to ensure you can complete the task. It is essential to understand the credentials of the individuals who you're planning to schedule, the preferences they have for scheduling and the length of time they've been working to ensure that you don't give the same person too little time while another is given too many. If you fail to follow one of these crucial actions, your schedule will be ineffective and you'll have to spend the large portion of your time trying to re-arrange your schedule in order to make sure that the job is completed. It's impossible to make a system work without having the required features.

Second, if the separate actions aren't compatible and aren't compatible and the system fails, it will fail. For instance, if , for example, you receive an email regarding an important meeting , and you alter the time and date using your computer, but the information isn't recorded and up-to-date on your phone or with other people who work with you it will cause problems. The meeting could be missed or have to call other people who expected to be able find you at the time of the meeting. Whatever the case the system is likely to disappointed you due to the fact that the various parts don't work together.

You've likely heard of synergy. It's the process whereby an amalgamation of elements results in an outcome that is more than the parts that are combined.

John Lennon and Paul McCartney are an excellent instance of synergy. Together, these two amazing musicians and songwriters made music that was better than anything they created independently. Your system of organization should result in synergy, which allows you to work more efficiently with the resources available than the resources you have on their own. It's like adding 2+2 to get five! If you're able to manage your tasks as well as Information, People and Time in the way that you are able to accomplish more and deliver better outcomes, your system of organization is in place. Since the various parts don't only function together, but are actually built on top of one another and your results will allow you to achieve more efficiently and in less time.

The strength of an equipment is that when it is set up it can produce results with a minimum of effort. Think of it as installing the water pump. Prior to the pump, you'd be required to go to the source of water (a river or any other source of water) to extract the water you require and then transfer it back to the place you wanted it. The water pump, on the contrary, brings your water using small effort. It takes much less effort to pump manually on the hand of the water pump, than go to the source of the water to transport it back. You'll have more water in a shorter time and at a lower cost. This is the advantage of a well-organized system. Once your system of organization is in place, it allows you to achieve more out of less. It will be less time-consuming to spend time searching for information, pondering what you're supposed do next, or trying to meet a deadline you didn't think about.

Systems function by laying out procedures which don't change. The repetition of a system can allow users to get proficient in the specific actions, so that they become routine. You don't need be thinking about it or exert effort to accomplish them. The more time you spend using the system, the more efficient it gets. However, that doesn't mean it will never change. Being adaptable is essential to having an effective system of organization. It's going to require updating or modified however, when the overall structure is established changing it is typically a straightforward process.

Organizational Philosophical

There are a myriad of thoughts and opinions on the value and importance of an organization system. We are not trying to convince you that there is a need to be organized, but rather to aid you in understanding the purpose of an organization. Being organized does not mean being perfect. Perfectionism is in many ways an opposite to organization. The goal of organization is to simplify life for you, making you more productive , and to ensure your tranquility. The pursuit of perfection often involves focusing on one thing until you've reached proficiency. Anyone is organized However, not everyone is an naturally well-organized person. While you must strive to develop an organization system that is beneficial to you, it will not be the best method of organization. A person with a natural aptitude to organize could easily enter your system and make improvements. This is fine, as we're not looking for perfect instead, we want to build an organization that you're content with, which improves your productivity as well as reducing your anxiety.

Productivity is crucial. It is the ability to accomplish more work done in less time. The aim of efficiency is being capable of producing high-quality work throughout the day. A lot of people believe that the task of organizing could reduce their productivity by requiring them todo, but this isn't true. The purpose of an organizing system is to reduce unnecessary steps, and to make available resources and increase your productivity. If you have a well-designed system for organizing you will be more efficient, so your ability to be productive is a crucial aspect of your plan. You must identify those actions that can increase your productivity and those that hinder people from being efficient. Your system of organization should eliminate the obstacles and give you users with the data that you require to be more efficient. It's not only about files or documents, as well; it could be that a particular kind of environment makes your work more efficient. Perhaps it's music, or perhaps peace and quiet. There are many aspects to think about when designing your system of organization.

The way you interact to the computer system crucial. For example, are the labels clearly visible on your files? What is the closest to hand you actually need them? Do you put your organizational elements near your desk or do you make them out of reach? There is no right or wrong answer the answer is based on your personal preferences and what is most meaningful to your own way of thinking. Your organization system must be easy to understand, that is, it will come as a natural. For instance, for some , getting up to go to a shared printer just doesn't make sense. They believe it's logical to have a printer in their work space, is the best method to increase their efficiency and allow them to put in their best efforts in their work.

When you create your organization system, efficiency not perfection is the best rule of the thumb. It should be easy to use with the way it's constructed and the way you interact with it. The system may not be active, but it should to feel like a well fitting shoe, comfortable and practical. Remember these ideas as you think about the ways you can create an organization system that is effective for you.

The Designing Your Organizational System

Through this book, we'll be working through concepts will be useful to incorporate into your system of organization. For instance , in Chapter 3 we'll look at your workspace. In Chapter 5, we'll talk about the management of time. We need to determine the elements that make an organization system function for you in particular. There are three elements that can be used to customize your organization that you can consider: your personality type as well as your working habits and your energy levels daily.

It is not obvious that your personality is a factor that affects not just the way you conduct yourself as well as the way you handle interactions, how you perceive your experience, and how you interact with others as well as information and difficulties. For example, someone with a drive personality is likely to lead an event and strive for perfection, whereas a more emotional personality seeks to avoid conflict or change. Your system of organization will reflect your personal style. There are a variety of online tools that can assist you in determining and understanding your personal style. For the purposes of this article, I'll divide them into four types, with the majority having a combination of two distinct kinds.

The first is the persona that drives. This kind of person is a fan to lead and is always looking for new ways to record-breaking and pursuing the best results. The second is the fun-loving personality. The person who is always seeking to have fun and is often seen as uninformed at times. They prefer leisure activities over anything else. The third is their calm personality. They are adamant about justice and friendship and prefer to be in crowds but do not want to be the leader. Then there is the melancholy persona. They don't enjoy changes or conflicts However, they are generally solid under pressure and reliable. Spend some time figuring out what kind of person you are and use the information you have gathered to make your system of organization fit your needs by incorporating your objectives, preferred style of work and your preferred working routines.

Another aspect to consider when designing your organization system is your personal work habits. Do you work more hard when you have a goal in mind or when you are given a clear job description? Do you think that you can be a creative person? Do you enjoy working in groups or on your own? Are you comfortable being part of a bustling workplace or do you prefer solitude? Are you more physically or mentally challenged? Are there tasks that are part of your work that drag you down and cause stress such as long meetings, hectic workschedules, and deadlines that are looming? Incorporating these aspects will make a significant impact on how you build your system of organization. A simple example is if you develop a system others can comprehend and use. For example, if you prefer to work in an organization, you shouldn't have an organizational structure that you only understand. You'd like an open system that everyone can join and contribute to, as well as improve. However If you prefer working on your own you are free to do whatever you like with your organizational layout.

Additionally, you must take into consideration your energy level. We all go through parts of our day that we are able to are more energetic, have better focus , and the ability to accomplish a lot of work accomplished. There are also preferences for the way we work during the day. It is possible that you prefer long, periods of uninterrupted time that enable you to focus You'll need to have a plan set that lets you "bank" the jobs that will require you away from your desk for example, making copies or completing reports. In contrast you may work better in short bursts, then you could set up a plan which takes you away from your desk frequently to let yourself take an opportunity to take a break. Also, you should consider the way you prefer to spend your day to plan your schedule. If you are in a specific area for the entire day without a reason to leave your office it is unlikely that you require an organized system that can be integrated with your phone, laptop computer, and tablet. However If you are always moving around attending meetings, getting together with clients or creating presentations, you'll need an organization system that is flexible and accessible even when you're far from your desk.

Remember these rules when we begin to look at the details of your job life and generating suggestions on how you can remain organized. Take time to determine your character. Create your own list of the ways you work best and your energy levels daily. By using this list as a starting point We'll go over the specifics of your work and assist you in creating a plan that is effective for you.

Chapter 3: How To Organize Your Work Space To Boost Productivity

After we've laid out the fundamentals and the importance of organization now we can start working towards getting organised at work. There are many aspects of organization we'll take into consideration, but the primary and most fundamental will be your work space. It doesn't matter the type of job you perform whether you're an executive in an office with a corner in a towering building or you could be one of the entry-level employees working on the factory floor. The work you do isn't nearly as important as the place you perform it. A majority of people have a specific space , and it says something about the person you are. Are you messy with files piles of papers stacked around your work area or desk? Do you have old documents and files that are a mess in your workspace? Are you having trouble finding details or maybe making enough room that you can work from?

Sometimes, we work in shared spaces , and the people we share space with, or maybe the people who came before us haven't done a an adequate job of staying organized. There may be files and boxes of work that are not being used, empty containers, spare parts and other materials that must be dealt with. No matter what the condition of your workspace, if you want to stay organized, you'll have to create an organization that will keep the tools you utilize frequently as well as the objects that you use regularly flow through your workspace efficiently and in an organized manner. This is a lot like the laundry room. Many homes have a space that is specifically designed for laundry. It is likely that you keep the items you require within that space like laundry detergent and bleach, as well as fabric softener and stain removal. You may have a method for segregating the laundry as it enters the space, separating it into similar colors , and setting up special settings for specific things. There is a system to move the clean laundry to where they belong, which could be hanging out in the closet or folded and stored away.

Your workspace should be set up the identical. Tools you utilize to complete your tasks on every day are all in your reach. You don't want to locate the laundry detergent at one side of your home and then search for your softener for your fabric on the other. It's easier when the materials that you require to get accomplished are in your reach and readily available. It doesn't matter if the tools include computer programs, staplers or hammers or screw drivers. Whatever job you're doing, you'll need the space to store your tools to complete the task.

You will need an organized system to move tasks into your workplace and then finishing the work and then transferring it into the space where it will go following. It is essential to keep track of and track any material such as documents, documents or other projects you are working on. It is essential to have a system of distinguishing between what's current and what's more dated as well as what is urgent and what needs until it is completed. It is essential to have a method for making sure that the files aren't confused, lost or lost. The arrangement of your workspace should facilitate this. It should be clear and easy to keep things tidy and it is easy to see in a glance the tasks you need to be doing at any given point. Let's explore some ways you can get your workspace tidy.

Making Use of Your Resources

One of the major issues with organization programs is that they are priced an enormous amount. Not only do you have to purchase this program but also the resources that they provide to assist you in using the program are also expensive. It's normal however, you don't need to spend an arm an arm to be organized. It's all about making use of what you already have. The first step to consider is making an inventory of all the things you use regularly. For example, do you have a desk, computer, office tools, equipment and more? You must know the things you have to work with, and what you'll need, and what you do not need. Create an inventory. Take a look through the drawers on your desk. The enemy of clutter is organizing and you've probably accumulated lots of it. It's moment to get rid of anything that is of no worth. It's time to make your home feel more like home But let's concentrate first on the basic things you'll require to get your job accomplished.

Once you have an understanding of the things you have and need, it's time to start considering what you'll require. If you have money to spare, Don't restrict your thoughts to particular items, but instead think about what this object is able to perform. It's possible that you require a new desk but chances are you'll be stuck with your current desk therefore let's maximize the use of it. Are there drawers? How about lighting? Is there a big computer that dominates the space? Consider the work you have to complete in this particular space. Are you using your computer often? Do you make use of pencils, markers, pens or highlighters? Do you create prototypes, create objects, and organize components? Whatever you are doing you do, there's a way for you to accomplish it efficiently Your workspace is a a major role in it.

Consider what you do the majority of your time on and look at what you might have to offer that could help. It might not be the tools you use, but there are sources that can assist you. Perhaps you have stackable papers tray, or a cup that can be used to store the writing tools or other writing equipment. It is possible that you could convert your cabinet into an minifiling cupboard, or turn a computer tracker tray to a neat storage space for office supplies.

If you've got a wall or cubical walls, you could make use of them to record important events you don't wish to forget. It is also possible to use wall mounted racks for filing to keep the track of your current projects. If you have a bookcase, you can use it as storage, and it can also help you keep records of important files and documents. Dry erase markers are excellent for storing important data. Some are equipped with metal backings to allow you to pin things up with magnets. There is also a wallboard in your local hardware store . It functions as dry erase boards. If you do not work on the computer and have a clock in your workspace, having it visible can aid you in making more of the time you spend.

Making Simple the Organization System Simple

The second tip for organizing your work space is to be simple. You don't want to fill your workspace with various organizing tools, but instead, you'll want to utilize the least amount of items you can. The more objects you be able to see, the more difficult it is to concentrate. Many people prefer to store items in places where they can easily be able to see them, so that they won't get lost in the dust. However, If you create a great method, you can get things out of view and allow your mind to concentrate on the work that is in front of you. There is no need to worry about being distracted by things because you're aware of where things you are working on currently are stored. Once you've finished one task, you'll be able to move directly onto the next.

Sometimes, workers must quit working during the middle of the course of a project. Maybe you need to wait for figures to be received from the department of accounting. Perhaps you're waiting for a vendor to submit their order and send you the supplies you require. Many people worry that if they store that work aside, they'll never recall to revisit it. A system of organization can eliminate the problem. Keep in mind that a great system is a system to accomplish work. It's similar to checking your email. You constantly refresh your mail page each when you check your email to ensure you don't miss any important messages. Once you've got your system in place each time you begin to work or complete your project, you'll need to examine the work-in-progress file or drawer to ensure that the unfinished projects aren't yet ready to be completed.

Another aspect of organization is that it is prone to becoming complicated. It is possible to start with a small amount of work however, as you become more focused on the way you organize your work, it's likely to expand, so keep in mind to keep in mind that the system you have created is still a work in progress. You can tweak it frequently to make it more efficient. The key is to continue simplifying. The more simple your system is the more likely to make use of it. If your system for organizing becomes complicated , you'll find yourself making a mess and before you know it, your work space is a mess.

There are four key elements of a basic organizational system. Although all four are essential but depending on the job you are in, you might not require all. You can eliminate the unneeded elements to make your layout as minimal as is possible. The first step is to create a space for your work. In many companies there is a tendency for the "to-do" tasks are more important than the amount of work we are able to do. Therefore, you'll require not just a work space but also a space to store your work. This is a space for tasks that need to be finished but haven't completed yet. The present work section is typically divided into urgent and the non-urgent work. It isn't a good idea for urgent work to be filed in the midst of projects that could be put off, so it could be beneficial to have two separate areas where your current work can move to.

The next step is to create some space to store projects you've started but not finished. There are a variety of reasons to not finish an assignment regardless of whether it's simply a task you had to complete towards the close in the course of the day. This is the one you always keep in your document, and it must be checked at the beginning of the day , or whenever there's a change in tasks. If you find resources which allow you to complete one of these projects , you must finish it as soon as possible. If you create a space for the unfinished projects and letting them go, you will be able to take them off your plate, forget about them, and not use your mental energy to keep them in mind. Even if you don't often are faced with projects that remain unfinished You should create some space just in the event that they do. The mere sight of the empty box or file will give you a confidence boost each time you go through it.

Thirdly, you'll need an area to store your work that you've just completed. In the case of your workplace there could be a time when you're at nearing the end of the road on certain projects or you might need to transfer them to another person. In some instances it could be the necessity to keep the project until the new person or team is ready. It is possible to divide the box or file into three parts, the work you have on file, the project that has to be transferred to the next division and the work you hold until the next stage is in place. For example, if you are employed by an architect's firm, you might need to submit your work to be printed and then to the team that follows. There might be an illustration of your concept or design. Alternatively, you may have to hold the work until the client has paid their fee. Sometimes, the plans are put off until a contractor can be found and the customer is prepared to submit the plans to the proper municipal office. Whichever the case, it is important to organize your work to monitor the work you've completed.

In the end, you should have an archive of the work once you're done with it. A backup, whether of the completed work once it's no longer required or the material you used to create the piece. For instance, a journalist could send their finished story to the editor, but should keep their sources in a safe place to be able to confirm some details in the future. The file does not have to be kept in a safe place always. Most likely, you won't require the things stored in your archive often however, with a well-organized space for this kind of work or resource it will be easier to keep them safe from being lost or let them clutter up your workspace.

Every item has a home and every Home is labeled

The last aspect of organizing your space is to ensure that every thing can be put into an appropriate, defined space. This is often the longest time, however it's crucial because of two reasons. In the first place, by making an area for each item you'll be able to quickly and quickly locate what you require and increase your productivity. When you put things aside, you'll feel satisfaction and satisfaction. You'll look at your workspace at end of each day and be feeling satisfied that your organization system is functioning. Another benefit is that when you put things aside, you'll be able to turn off an emotional switch that lets to stop working, so that you are completely engaged with your loved ones and family even when you're off work. The act of putting your things away, even the project you're working on (it is placed in the unfinished work file or in the box) and seeing a neat area will put your mind at relaxed. You'll be able to see that everything should be where it's supposed to be, so you don't have to be concerned about it. It'll be waiting to greet you upon your return , and it will take only a small period of energy and time to come on track, whether you're just heading to bed for the night or going on vacation.

It is not necessary to purchase labels or an attractive sign on every item, but it can assist in labelling things. The boxes or files you keep include some sort of label to help you see immediately what belongs where in your work space. Labels may not be necessary to indicate the locations where your paperclips or pencils are located however, if others are using the space you have created, labeling can help them locate what they require and help them put things back where they belong.

It is also helpful to write your name on things that are prone to being borrowed , but not returned. If your book or stapler is engraved with your name upon it, the person who borrowed it is reminded each whenever they come across it that they must return the item to you. Labels also aid in identifying areas you don't frequent. In other words, you might not be able to complete a task however having the space labeled available will allow you to trust that your organization system will be ready for whatever situation you have to face. In time, you'll be comfortable with where things go and will not require labels, but as we're just at the beginning, you should take your time and label items that will help you stick to your organization.

Now that you've set up your workspace we can move on to managing the hard-copy documents.

Chapter 4: Fast And Easy Way To Handle Hard Copies

The most important need individuals face when it comes to organizing is managing the hard copy of their documents. We have a technology that allows every day work can be completed electronically, however in the majority of enterprises, there's the need to deal with a plethora of paperwork that includes important files, memosand announcements, newsletters and reports. Many are handed over through departments from one one branch to another while others are left on your desk , waiting to find to find a place. A lot of people have many piles of paperwork on their desks. The piles are moved around and moved about, but are rarely addressed. The mere appearance of your workstation could create an increase in stress levels. A messy workspace conveys that your job is stressful chaotic, messy and never-ending. A messy desk can make you feel as if you'll never catch up with all the tedious and difficult tasks that drain your energy and takes the enjoyment from your work. Compare that feeling with a clean and tidy workspace. Your workspace will be neat, inviting and free of stacks. It doesn't mean that you won't have papers at your workstation, however each object will be put in the appropriate areas and there'll be plenty of workspace so that you begin your day ready to complete lots of work accomplished and end your day satisfied with the results you've achieved.

It's crucial to take the ideas in the book and tailor the concepts to your specific circumstances. There may be a lot of paperwork, or perhaps just some. There could be items that are a mess in your work space and scraps of materials, samples or your own materials that do not have a proper home. In some cases, particularly if your schedule is incredibly busy and you're trying to keep up with everything you have to do can become stressful. So let's explore the steps to stay on top of every job you do to ensure that it is in order and available at moment's notice.

One Size doesn't fit all

Particularly when it comes to the way you organize your hardcopies, materials or work materials the same size won't work for every. It is possible that you have a coworker working at the same desk working in the same way and having the similar amount of clutter, however, you'll probably arrange things differently. What you're looking for is what you prefer. The first step is to identify the "items" you're constantly working with. What kind of materials are you seeing piled all around you in the workplace? Editorial staff might have books and manuscripts while a manufacturer could possess scrap materials and tools. It is equally important to be organized for an accountant as florists, to fast food chef as it is to the investment banker. Everybody has "stuff" to manage. We call these items hard copies because most people own paper connected to their work that gets thrown away in their workspace.

After you have identified the clutter in your workspace, you can begin to categorize them. The majority of people work with three different types of work. One is the work that is assigned to them. For many people , this might include reports, files or any other type of paperwork. You may receive work orders electronically however, it's your responsibility to make hard copies when you've completed your task. No matter how you receive assignments, they should be regarded as to be in one class. Then, you must consider the tools you employ for your work. These could be office tools such as pens, paper clips and staples, or it could be actual tools such as chisels bolts, hammers, and hammers. Everything you require to perform your job or to use during your day is a different class. There are also personal items, ranging from photos and snacks to books and magazines to your mobile phones and headphone. Every one of them is essential however, let's focus on your personal belongings.

Your personal items are very important. They add your character and interests to your work. You're not a machine and shouldn't be expected to be one. Instead, you should possess some things that help you feel in your own home. If your work space reflect your personality, you'll perform better and be more productive. At present, take the time to put everything aside. Bring a bag home or a container and place them all in one location. Then, you'll bring them out again and place them the center of attention, once your work supplies and objects have home. You must think about the continuity and flow of your work space, therefore removing personal belongings will enable us to give each object a home. which means that personal belongings are merely an accent.

Let's look at the items to be worked on. What are they going to do when they arrive? They should be able to land in a designated area. Everything that enters your workplace needs to be placed in a landing area. There aren't many new projects at times that are most convenient for us. Most of the time, we're engaged in one task and might have many more waiting for new projects to arrive. There must be a designated area in your office to take on new assignments. It shouldn't be necessary to stop what you're doing to figure out which area it belongs to. It could be a piece of mail that must be separated, opened, and taken care of. It could be a memo or an old file you'll have to reference on the basis of a particular project. It could be a document that requires to be recorded and archived. Whatever it is , put it in the correct area until you are able to look through the things and then put them back in their appropriate areas. You can set aside some times throughout the every day to check the new items that are on the desk.

However, by putting them in the exact spot which is designated for them, you won't need to be concerned whether you'll lose any one of the things, and your productivity will improve because your work doesn't get interrupted every time a new thing arrives at your desk.

We've discussed briefly the importance of having a designated space for your current work, work that is not completed and work that you've completed. This is the time to locate those spaces and make sure that they're clearly marked. There must be an area to store those items that often make their way to your work space. If you look through the paper copies you have at the bottom of your desk You can put them in the right place. There is no way to say that one size will suit all, so let the effort. It could be necessary to have a location to reference your documents, or you might require a space to store client files that require to be accessible. Whatever you handle on a an ongoing basis, you should build your system around it.

Find a new home for the various tools you are using every day. Each item should be easily accessible However, this does not mean it must be on the desk or on a work space. Make use of the space you have available: shelves, wall hangers or cabinetry in close proximity. The aim is to keep these things in your possession in order to be able to utilize them, and then store them aside. They are crucial to accomplishing your tasks however they don't need to be a mess. Find a suitable home for each object. This will help you ensure that you have the right supplies. When you're surrounded by items an unorganized workspace, you won't know if you've got another pen, or if it's been taken out of. There may be several open boxes of half-used materials scattered all over the place and covered with other objects however, If you have a dedicated space to store your tools for work, you'll be able to see quickly how much you have, and whether you're in need of more. Also, you'll not spend searching for the items you require to increase your efficiency.

Let's go back to the personal items. It's not quite time to put away all your hardcopies however now that each thing has a place while your work flow is streamlined and efficient, you are able to swap out your personal items. If you're surrounded by lots of photos or other items that are placed on your desk and you need to establish the system of rotating. In some cases, you only have room to display one or two photos however, you could have four kids, in this case, you can set up two or three pictures, and then set a date (perhaps towards the time of day, for example friday) to rotate the existing images with two new pictures. Also, you need room for other things that aren't in your desk. They may not have to be on the desk as your other hard copies, however they must be accessible from your workspace.

Alphabetical against Chronological

It is the next stage to arrange every space you've identified. For example the file or work pending box your work pending file, tasks must be organized in a manner that lets you see what's most important. Based on the work you do you will need to determine the best way to organize important information. Many individuals have deadlines, and prefer to organize actions according to the project's due date. For example, if there is a task which needs to be finished by Tuesday and the other must be completed by Friday, then the Tuesday task should be filed before the Friday work. You could arrange the files according to the order they arrive to ensure that the first task to arrive in the front while the final job you receive is put in the back. In this way, when you tackle the tasks from front to back, you'll complete them in the exact way they were received. This is known as chronological order. It is commonly used for jobs where time is an issue. It is also utilized in situations where projects or projects are completed, and then transfer to another stage of work or an additional department.

If you're on the other side you are working on recurring projects or client files that you return to repeatedly it is advisable to store items in alphabetical order. This way, you can locate the file quicklyand without having to go through each file until you locate the one you want. Alphabetical files are utilized for work that you perform or the resources you use are related to a single client or project, and typically when you're the one maintaining the physical copies for the long-term.

Every method to organize your files comes with its own advantages and you must arrange your files according to the method that is most beneficial for you. For those who have a large number of hard copies for every project or job can organize their files in chronological order however, the contents of the documents could be organized according to alphabetical sequence. Make sure you use what works for you. Your coworker might work one way while you work in a different way. It's fine, so it's a matter of making your sense, and you're comfortable with the method you work.

How to organize files

The majority of digital copies are deposited as files. Your organization system could include files for specific types of work or in progress. There are some tips that are crucial in the process of organizing your documents. We'll look at these and offer tips on how to implement the most effective methods to ensure that your organization system is effective for you.

The first step is to mark your documents. It's surprising how many people do not bother with the labeling step. The reason is that they usually start with a small amount of data and already have an idea of where they are. When they have to update their data, they can browse through the files and see what's contained in each. The problem is the time, the more you keep using files, the more complicated they become. If you don't have labels, there's a good chance that you have similar files spread across multiple files. Also, it's a safe bet your hard-copy copies of your documents aren't in any kind of order. In the end, this inefficiency can cost you not just time, but also money. It could result in you losing papers or important documents, and wasting your time. Make the effort now to label your documents. Imagine how simple for you to organize documents and search for anything you need if you could look through your drawer or cabinet in a flash. Labeling is easy and most files are equipped with marking materials. Spend 20 minutes labeling all your files in a clear and systematic manner.

You'll also need your files accessible. There may be a file drawer on your desk however, if not, you need to purchase a small filing cabinet for your office. The most important rule to remember for files is to not overflow them. If you have lots of hard copies to manage, you must create files that are based on the smallest common denominator. The biggest hurdles in keeping your files to date is when your files are messy and overflowing it's similar to trying to arrange the home of a hoarder. Nobody wants to look through piles and piles of unorganized, out of current documents. It's important to organize your files in a simple manner and use an archive to make sure that your files aren't overcrowded.

Archives are those files that are no longer being used or are not used often. Archives can be created just like your existing files however they don't need to be in the same location. Also the archives don't have to be part of your work space. Archives are valuable and should be kept and used but they're not an ongoing requirement. You could also create an "To

Archives" file or box to keep your finished projects into and only send the hard copies to your archives after you've got enough.

Here are some easy actions to follow when you've got an idea of how to arrange your hard-copy files. If you do have an existing file system, make sure it's compatible to your overall design. If you don't already have a file system, start with one. It's an excellent method to organize all work-related materials that you own. It doesn't require an entire filing cabinet in order to organize your documents either. You can find a smaller plastic filing sleeve for filing at every office supply retailer. These basic organizational tools are easily portable and come in a range of sizes that will simplify your work for your. After that, you should look through all of your documents that you can be able to fit into a file. There may be a mountain of paperwork or some drawers filled with odd and end-of-the-line items, however, any hard copies are in your possession must be organized and easily accessible. We'll discuss electronic filing and organizing in chapter 6.

Also, ensure that each item that you work with is clearly marked for it. The goal should be to create a working space that is designed for the highest effectiveness. Many times, when people hear the words they believe that their work space can't be enjoyable or even contain personal belongings, but this isn't the reality. You just need to be the king of your own domain and ensure that each item is in a place where you will be able to get to it quickly and have enough space to get the job completed, and also are able to identify the next step after you've completed the task. Let's now look at strategies to manage your time.

Chapter 5: How To Manage Your Time To Do More With Less Stress

A good time management technique is a form of art. We all have the exact amount of time each day, however some are able to get more accomplished than others. The good thing is that you can be an expert in time management by incorporating the right techniques to your routine.

Time management isn't a problem. It's really simple, but it requires a different way of looking at your day. The majority of people think that they are going through the challenges and activities of the day as if a fish swims across the stream. People who excel in managing their time see their lives differently. They view each minute an opportunity. While many people think of slow moments in their work as a refreshing break away from their seemingly never-ending task ahead, those who manage their time effectively make the most of every minute that they have. If we return to the fish analogy you'll see a lot of people swimming between big rocks to large rock. They battle with the flow until they locate tiny pockets of water that's not pushing them back into the stream. They take refuge within the safety of the rock for as long as they canand then set out to find another site to rest. In the workplace, this is akin to breaks, talking around the water fountain and doing a bit of internet surfing each time they log on to do some work-related job.

Being a successful managing time doesn't mean you don't have time for pleasure or that you have to work all day long. Instead, the best time managers work on their own the stream. They seek ways to accomplish their tasks faster as well as with lesser effort. They make the most of time and conditions when they can or are at their maximum efficiency or perform any more effective work. Take this as an example: Rolland comes into the office at a certain hour every day because mornings are a prime moment in his energy level. There is also a quiet atmosphere in the office during this time. After people have gotten to work, the majority of them are in bed in their work, checking emails, or reading news articles on the internet. Rolland is able to accomplish more during the initial two hours of unrestricted work than he does at any other time during the day. Another important aspect of his work is calling potential clients, which is what he does while waiting for his team members to get ready for the meetings that which he must take part in. He is focused throughout the meetings, but he also makes an agenda of things to be completed in the event that the meeting is off the mark or isn't entirely concerned with his work. The rest of the day follows the same pattern as the rest of us, but He is able to get more accomplished in less time. He also departs early than the rest of us. Rolland is a skilled time-manager because he adheres to some simple rules for example, establishing a daily routine that is suited to him, and making the most of his downtime. Let's examine these concepts in greater detail , and consider how they apply to your life.

Organising Your Daily Routine

A majority of our days are alike. They do the same things every day or every week. You're likely to have an established routine, whether you realize that or not. The majority of people don't make the most of the options they have to make the most of their daily routine. Let's take a look at your energy levels daily and then focus on planning your day to ensure that you have time to people, meetings as well as phone calls for work.

Your energy level throughout the day is comprised in the spirals, ups and downwards that you encounter throughout the day. Many people believe that they are more energetic, have more concentration and motivation to work at specific time during the day. On the other hand, they can also experience moments when they feel exhausted or unfocused, and are not productive. One of the best methods to make the most of productivity is to identify the cycle of your energy and alter your routine so you maximize the value of your day.

A lot of people feel more energetic when they begin their day, usually about mid-morning. Also, many suffer from an afternoon slump, an ache or sluggishness that strikes around an hour or so following lunch, and may last until late in the afternoon. Many people believe in the false notion that productivity is being at work and trying to rebalance their power cycle to get results throughout the day. This is not true since it actually sabotages not just your energy levels but also your feelings about the work you do. It is best to do the most important tasks at times of high energy and perform monotonous, tedious work at the lower points. It is helpful for many people to keep the work which require them to get off their desks during those moments of low energy. The thing that most people don't know is that when you sit for long periods even when you're extremely busy at work your body begins to fall into a sleep state. The mind is then challenged with focus and effectiveness. If you can identify ways to align your daily routine to your energy levels and get more accomplished since your mind and body are in the same place. When you get up and move around , you'll keep your circulation running at a constant level and your body's chemical balance will be in better equilibrium, which can reduce the periods of lulls, and ensure that you're functioning at or near to your highest levels of energy all day long.

Once you know your daily energy level and your daily routine, you can match it according to your cycle. Do not attempt to complete challenging work when you're experiencing an energy deficit. Do not waste the time of meetings and chattering with colleagues during your peak energy periods. What people often don't know is that when they try to complete work during low energy levels, they can become annoyed and angry about their work. They become anxious about the daily chores and despise their work. If they align their work schedule to their energy levels and get more accomplished with less effort and they'll look at their job in a completely different perspective. They'll not feel guilty about socializing with their colleagues since they're more accomplished during high-energy times, and when they're at work socializing, they realize it's the time of day and that they won't get enough done. Their performance at work will also improve and they'll start to receive more attention and maybe even increase their standing. The advantages of taking the time to study your daily routine and to adjust your daily routine are many and will immediately have an impact on your professional career.

After you've taken charge of your day-to-day schedule, it is time to start assigning specific times to certain tasks. Based on the job you are in, you could have to deal with coworkers and potential clients or individuals who influence your work. The issue with dealing with people is that it's extremely ineffective. It's not easy to gauge the results you get from developing a rapport with potential clients however it's essential for you to be able to convert them into a client. It is inevitable to have to deal with chatty colleagues or superiors who move throughout the office to speak with you. The goal is to determine times throughout your working day when you can get off your workstation and engaging with other people can be beneficial to you. If you visit your boss and tell them about your day at a time that is most convenient to you, then they will not visit you without warning. The coworkers will realize that you don't have a social life when you're at work and will not spend their time arguing with you. You'll also realize that you're spending precious energy-dense time talking to others which means you'll be experiencing interruptions more quickly as you become more adept at managing your time more effectively.

Meetings are an essential evil. There are very few businesses that know how to conduct a successful and efficient meeting. It is easy to get caught up with meetings that degrade the efficiency of your employees and disrupt the natural cycle of energy. From a casual meeting with a prospective customer or a strategic meeting of department leaders, it is important to be aware of how you manage your time during meetings. There are three steps you can do. The first is to arrive prepared for every meeting. You should have the answer to all questions, and keep your statistics and facts in your pocket. Establish a model of efficiency and organization , so that when you offer a suggestion regarding format changes (which is what you'll do naturally) people will pay attention. Then, you must learn to conduct a successful meeting. When you respect the time of others and get the desired results, they'll return to you over and over again, from customers to bosses. It is essential to learn how to manage meetings with your participants effectively and for many , that involves learning the fundamentals of facilitating a successful meeting. Even if you're not the person in charge of any meeting you must be knowledgeable the basics of running a great meeting to be able to offer sound suggestions. Also, you must make the most of your time at meetings effectively. Don't just sit around waiting for the discussion's topic or agenda to suit you. You must help lead and steer the discussion, or else you'll get things done while waiting. Make an agenda of the tasks you need to accomplish, and make changes to your schedule, or even note down the how decisions are taken.

Calls to the phone are yet another way to kill time. When it comes to making calls or making them if you are not being prepared and organized in advance, phone calls will ruin your productivity. Here are some suggestions to keep you in control of your phone time management. Start by establishing some time in your week or daily schedule to call. When you're calling back someone and making cold call, it is important to set aside a certain amount of time when you will be available to make calls. Based what the purpose of the calls as well as the way you feel about them, it is possible to plan the time into your high or low time, to ensure you are getting the results you want. For instance, if you only have to do is answer many calls per day, you could schedule this into your leisure time and use your peak energy for tasks that require greater concentration. However, if making calls is crucial to your job, you might want to schedule calls when you are energetic and engaged.

The second step to do is keep a notepad along with a pen beside your mobile. Each time you speak to someone , you must keep notes. Record the contact details, name of the person as well as the purpose of the conversation. This will allow you to keep track of calls, while keeping your attention on the primary reason for the call. Don't make calls to personal friends whenever you can. Calls from friends and family eat away at your time and take away of your focus. Some calls cannot be prevented However, by setting a precedent that you'd prefer to not to make these calls, you will increase your productivity at work.

Scheduling System

Scheduling is a different method to optimize the efficiency of your schedule. You must be able to plan your tasks to are compatible with your routine at appropriate times, and you should also be able to get your system to automatically update. There's nothing worse than having to make adjustments to your schedule using different devices, when you might be able to get something productive accomplished. Let's explore the best ways to create a scheduling system that is as efficient as you can.

The first step is to have an official calendar. It could be printed on paper , however electronic calendars are typically more effective. They are able to link the devices in a way that ensures the data isn't lost during the process of transfer. The central calendar should be in your pocket for the large portion of time. when you are spending the majority of your time in your office then you could make use of an application for your calendar that is on your computer's desktop or laptop, however if always on the go, you may prefer using your smartphone or tablet computer. The aim is to have a space that you can quickly and easily check what's happening at any given moment. Sometimes maintaining your schedule on your mobile phone is a bit of a hassle because you don't have the ability to view individual appointments as as you could with a larger device. Whatever method you decide to use, make sure you have set the time and time frame to each scheduled appointment. Take note of your routines and make sure the time you set for your appointment or meeting will allow you to complete the most work done throughout the remainder of the day.

Also, you need to organize your calendar in like you organized the hard copies. There will be meetings, appointments, deadlines, and presentations that are all mixed up which is why you require the ability to understand the events on your calendar in one glance. The majority of calendar software allows the use of colors to distinguish between personal and work occasions, or between clients and company-related meetings. Make use of the alarm feature to remind you of deadlines that are coming up and important appointment times. It's not a ploy to let your calendar software to help you track your activities. A well-designed calendar will let you input this information in order to not need to remember it every time. It is also possible to input blocks of time for working on specific tasks. For example, if you are required to deliver a presentation to a prospective client, when you've scheduled the presentation, make sure you go ahead and block time to practice your presentation or make improvements to the presentation. By scheduling time for crucial tasks, it allows you to manage your time, and helps you avoid getting over-scheduled.

It is also possible to break down tasks in your schedule into groups. For example, if, for instance, you're able to incorporate time into your schedule to do tasks outside of your desk such as copying or filing your archives, you could plan other activities to take care of even when you're away from your desk. So when you check your calendar, you will determine what you'll need to be doing at that point. Another instance is to make phone calls. There is lists of calls that have to be made, which you can use when you're at a loss or are forced to leave your desk. In the case of a traffic jam, you could be stuck in traffic, but if have a list of phone calls that have to be made, you can make the time.

Also, make sure that all of your devices are synced and update on a regular basis. It's no good to set up an appointment on your mobile if the appointment doesn't show up when you log into your PC. In the same way, you don't want to run one program on your laptop as well as another one on your phone It is best to make use of the same software across all platforms and even at home to ensure that you are in sync with all your tasks. Cloud storage is an excellent way to gain the ability to access your files any time. Cloud storage lets you upload your files to a secure server and can access it wherever you have the Internet connection. Cloud storage is a fantastic method to store everything together, regardless of whether you are working at the office, at home , or while on the go.

We've now looked at the practical methods to organize the time you have, we'll take a look at how you can arrange all your online content.

Chapter 6: Digital Organization Strategies For Rapid Access To Information

Staying current with the content you have on your computer is an essential aspect of any organization's design. It is essential to connect your digital content alongside your hard copies as well as other resources. As more the work is being done with smartphones, computers tablets, and other digital sources, you'll require an effective system for keeping the track of your documents and files to ensure that your items aren't lost.

The computer you have installed is set in a way that allows you to organize documents in folders, much as the filing cabinet. Every computer is constructed layers upon layers in order to let you access every file you require in a matter of clicks. The issue for many is that they don't have a idea of how to connect their files with the basic concept of an electric signal. You aren't able to grasp it, touch it or put it away in a drawer. It's vital and if you don't have the foresight and preparation your digital data could be lost in the chaos. There's been many stories of people who lost their computer or stolen, struck by lightning, or simply crashed. If they weren't able to have their data saved recently it is likely that they lost a significant amount of work. Organising your digital content not only helps you locate what you require when you require it, but can also allow you to connect it seamlessly between your digital devices as well as your hard copy files , too. Imagine the possibility of having a system to back your work in a way that is automatic or you are able to access from any location. What about an organization system that's based on your computer? We'll look at everything and more in this article. Don't believe that since the large portion of work you do is online that you're automatically organized. Keep in mind that organizing helps you find and gain access to Tasks, People, Information & Time. Digital content isn't any different from other content that you do and must be organized to ensure that it can be used for your benefit too. Let's take a look at some ways you can keep track all of the content you create online.

Connecting Your Devices

The first step to organize your digital media is to connect your devices. In essence, every device you use for computing needs to be able to talk with each other and exchange information. There are a variety of methods to accomplish this, and we'll cover three options, cloud computing as well as creating an internet-connected network, and using identical software. Since technology is constantly evolving rapidly, it is essential to keep abreast of the most current information to make the right choices regarding what kind of hardware and software you'll require to ensure that your organization is running at its best. Some developments are not essential, but by staying up to date with the latest developments you'll be able make difficult decision of the best time to upgrade, and the things you shouldn't have. Let's take a look.

Cloud computing, or online storage is quickly getting to be the standard for a lot of users when it comes to connecting their devices. A database online for your entire information is a useful tool to keep you well-organized. Consider it an archival building that is a constant companion to you. You can access the data within the "cloud" anytime at any time, day or night, anywhere in the world , as long as you have access to the internet. Naturally, these are great apps for those who travel frequently or work at home and at their workplace. One of the advantages organizationally related to cloud computing is the fact that all of your devices have access to the same data.

Although the cloud does not connect all your gadgets at once, it allows users to store data in one location using one device, then access it with another. For example, you could write an outline at work on your desktop computer, however later download the presentation for an official trip and present the presentation via tablets. If, on the other hand, your software for organizing is cloud-based, then it is possible to modify the program and then connect or update every device you use. For example, if your scheduling software is online-based and you are online to update, access and modify it, every time you create an appointment it is updated. To make changes to your schedule on every gadget, you have to do is access the internet and save the most recent changes.

A crucial step to network your devices is using the identical software across all of your devices. There are many devices you can have, including desktop computers or tablet computer, laptop or smart phone.

There is a chance that you own more than one of them between your personal devices as well as those that you use at work. In many cases, we look for bargains and end up buying gadgets from various manufacturers which run on various operating systems. It is good to know that the majority of software is compatible with different devices, so even though your devices may use distinct languages and operate various ways, you will usually locate software that works across all devices. If you use the same program, you can ensure that any file or document you work with on one device is readable or modified and used with any other. Certain software can create compatible versions of the work you create However, often the documents will be modified during the conversion process and cause your headaches when you attempt to alter files. Furthermore, you'll be restricted in the things you can alter and how information flows between one device to another. If you use the same program on each device, you will be sure that the work you do will be identical across all devices and any modifications made will be implemented quickly and effortlessly. Your integrity and the quality of your work will be assured and security is well worth making sure your devices have the identical software. The software will not connect to your device, yet you are able to transfer your work across your devices via cloud-based storage or email.

The most efficient way to connect all of your devices is to create an internet-connected network. Wireless networks are quite common but what a lot of people aren't taking advantage of is the access you have with different devices that are connected to one network. If you go to the settings for your network device to enable file sharing. Make sure that your device is completely accessible, which means every device connected to the same network (that means that it's turned off and connected to internet via wireless) is able to be used from every other gadget. In this way, you are able to access a document that has been saved to a different device, edit it and save it on several devices. For instance, you could use a calendar software installed on your desktop computer on your workstation. When you're in the course of a meeting, you could access this program on your tablet computer. You can also include the most recent business trip that your boss has just assigned to you. Then, save the updated calendar on your desktop computer, tablet computer, as well as your laptop computer. There isn't any need to do anything else, the program was changed across all devices in one move.

Incorporating Organizational Programs

It doesn't require an expert on computers to manage your digital devices and contents. Actually there are plenty of organization software programs available for computers available. Instead of creating a new system it is better to buy one of the programs, and install it on your various devices, and use it to help you organize your work. Many of them offer tips on how you can create an organization system to organize your work space and hard copy documents as well. Here are some suggestions to take into consideration when you are integrating an organization program onto your computer.

Perhaps the most crucial aspect of any system, whether computerized or not to be, is whether it matches your personal style and your strengths. The last thing you'd like to avoid is one that is so rigid that it can't be modified to suit your needs and work way of life. If the system makes you feel frustrated or leaves you feeling oppressed, it's not the best fit for you. You want an application that's designed to make you feel confident when you use it. It must provide you with tools you need to complete more in less time and effort. You must be able to manage your tasks as well as people, information and time in a way that is logical to you.

Additionally, the system must be compatible with the job you're in. Many people pick excellent organizational software that aren't suited to their particular job setting. You don't want a program that creates a challenge for you. It's not a good idea to have an arrangement that's too complicated or cannot be modified to suit your needs. If the system you're using has you performing four steps , when you could complete the identical task in just two steps, it's time to look for a different software. The program makers often develop their programs to meet the needs of the largest, most complicated organizations. You must select a program that meets your needs and helps make your job simpler.

Also, you must ensure that the software you are using will work on all of your devices. In certain situations you might not be allowed to install the program on more than one device , or when you're using various types of devices, the program could run on one device, however not on other devices. If you find that you're unable to access or use the program when you are on the move as well as at your home choose a different application. Imagine your organization system as a way to streamline your daily life, bringing your work, your interests and personal life into the same direction. It should maximize your strengths and enable you to use the organizational system in any circumstance.

You should also be aware of the cost. There are many programs that have an initial price however, they will charge you for the privilege of installing it on multiple devices , or include ads-on's and upgrades you are taught to use, but cost you an additional fee to enable access to the program. The last thing you want to put your time and effort learning to make use of an organizational system that isn't affordable.

Organizing Your Email

Most people will find one of the least organized areas of their lives is their email accounts. They may have important emails from coworkers mixed with junk emails. There may be emails from potential clients that get lost in their mailers. It's not uncommon for important emails to be deleted or misplaced. The result could be a significant amount of time and energy wasted and the costs of losing clients.

It doesn't matter what email software you are using for your email, from office-based programs to free email apps on the internet They all share some features that they share. One of the most beneficial feature is the usage of folders. It is possible to create folders in the program to organize your emails. Imagine it as an organizer cabinet can be used to keep track of important documents. If you receive an email sent by your employer, you might not want to erase the memo after reading it, but in the end, your inbox will be full of mail. The process of finding that memo or any other email in particular, can be extremely difficult and stressful. When you create folders, you can go through an important email and put it in a folder where you are sure to locate it in the future, and not allow the inbox stuffed with messages. It might sound easy but a few minutes of organizing and cleaning up your emails will bring about a significant improvement in your efficiency and general impressions of your work.

Another problem in managing your email is the issue of spam. One company is capable of selling your email address , and in no time you'll be receiving a lot of junk mail that you don't want. Your email application should include spam filters to block unwanted messages, however sometimes , it fails to filter the spam that you don't want, or prevents you from receiving the messages you want to see. It is essential to take just a quick scan of your email before you delete. It only takes about a minute, but it's more important when you perform it on a regular basis. It also ensures that you don't miss any important information. Do not open any unsolicited junk mail even if you think it's intriguing. Sometimes, just opening an email could unleash malware that can destroy your computer , or cause it to slow and reduce your productivity.

Making use of apps and sharing files

Another method of staying organized is to integrate applications into your organization design. Apps are software applications that usually focus on completing a single task. While an organizational program is designed to handle everything the job, an app functions more of a tool which helps your business run more smoothly. There are a myriad of business applications and more are being designed each day. The first apps were designed to be used on smart phones, but they are now available on tablets laptops, desktop computers and laptops as well. Apps can aid users in a variety of ways, and, in the majority of cases, they're fairly inexpensive. You might, for example, install the dictation application for your phone if you frequently send texts or struggle to use the smartphone keyboard difficult. Although the app might not be accessible on all of your gadgets, when it can save your time as well as makes your job more efficient when using your smartphone, it's an excellent option to consider using. A different example could be an "To-Do" app that lets you to create lists (from work-related checklists to lists for shopping) from one platform, classify these, prioritize them, and then distribute them to all of your devices in only one click. Utilizing apps lets users to modify their digital workflow and use time saving software to get the results you desire from your professional career.

Sharing files is another excellent method of organizing your digital files. If you do not keep all your digital files in one space, such as an online storage service that is accessible from anywhere across all your devices, then you need to take a look at file sharing. By changing the settings of your devices, you can save copies of your newly created work on all the devices you have. The best part about sharing files is the fact that you do not need to share all of your files. For example, if you write reports, you may not require that document on your smartphone or tablet. However, if you're involved in a project that is long-term, there might be several files you need access to across all of your devices. You could save one file to this device and another one to be shared. Once your devices are connected to each other, they change the information on a regular basis. If you're making use of cloud storage services, sharing files can be an ideal way to stay on top of your work, especially when you aren't connected via the Internet. For instance , you could work during a long journey when the data you need is stored on your laptop. When you use file sharing, your computer has been set to automatically share these files with all your other devices. If you return to your office and sync your laptopwith your office computer, it will transfer the files you made during the flight. It will do this automatically. This is a win-win situation in terms of productivity and can keep you organized too.

Chapter 7: Easy Ways To Stay Current In Important Business Communication

The biggest barriers to our productivity and organizational targets can be the telephone. This is a problem that we have no control over but it shouldn't be overlooked. How can you handle communications issues that don't match your design for organization?

The first thing to remember is that you shouldn't let your phone ruin your system. Every person has their own needs regarding phone calls. It is possible that you work in an environment where calling isn't a part of the job description, but you might find that your phone will not stop in its ring. Perhaps your job calls you to the phone all day. It is important to view the phone as an additional source for incoming information. Imagine it as an airplane. Your workspace is an airport.

Phone calls will be able to land, and offload data, before receiving information from you, and then returning to the airport. There must be a location to receive calls that will allow users to both be heard and hear. You require a system to manage important information as well as the integration of this information into your overall system. Also, you need to establish boundaries so that the amount of information or volume of communications doesn't take over your.

There are numerous methods of communication these days such as email, phone texts, or even instant messaging. There is a possibility of dealing with online teleconferencing using software such as Skype. Even if you remain firm and allow calls to go to voicemail, you will need to answer those calls in the end. So , how you handle the communication process is crucial. Communication skills can be an enormous difference in the outcome, or between being perceived to be someone dependable and reliable and one who isn't. But the good news is that you are able to handle it. Similar to all your other goals for organization, it requires time and effort on the front end , but when you put the effort into your communication, it will be well-organized and efficient which will give you an advantage over your colleagues and boosts your career.

Staying up to date with Important Information

One of the toughest challenges for people who struggle with being unorganized is that they are unable to keep up with all the data being transmitted through the channels of communication. If it's a face-to face meeting with their boss or a call perhaps even an email message, they are prone to forgetting. There are times when they want to appear knowledgeable and competent in interpreting and acting on something however, they get lost in the maze of work that they're stuck in. Since there is no organized system and they're constantly beginning and stopping or thinking of another thing that must be completed. When they get started it is easy to forget things they haven't had a copy of, yet they consider the process of keeping notes as work and they're busy enough with their lives as it is. If you take anything from this book, it ought to be this: write tasks down! Note-taking tasks down isn't an indication of weakness, it's actually very intelligent. If you're not a fan of write, you can download an application for dictation for your phone and simply record what you've heard, or the things you have to remember to complete. Most of the time, you can send yourself the note, and then include it on the "To-Do" to-do list.

Note-taking tasks helps you get the details out of your head , allowing your mind to concentrate on other things instead of being constantly distracted by the tasks you must complete. Keep a notepad or pencil handy every day. If you are in conversations on the phone, you should always note down the conversation. It is important to note the person you're talking with (first as well as last) as well as contact details in case it is pertinent as well as any other information you'll need to recall from the call. Now you have a hard copy to handle. If you try to recall what you were told the information doesn't match with your organization plan. You'll forget it or you'll be forced put off other important tasks to ensure you don't forget about it. In either case, it could affect your organization productivity, job performance and productivity.

If you write a reminder to yourself, you can solve the issue. It's possible to do this with any relevant information you receive. It could just be an idea or suggestion that you record in a safe place to allow you to return to the idea or even consider it in the future. For example the CEO might tell you that when your company starts expanding into neighboring states that she would like to work with an agency for real estate or agent. Based on the size of your business expansion, this could take an extended period of time, possibly even for years. It is likely that you won't be able to be able to recall that information. However, if you record it down, it'll transform into an actual reminder you can store and then forget about. And when it is time it is possible to return to the document and use the data. When you write it down, you won't need to think about it anymore and you'll be armed with the data in case you need it to ensure that you can act upon it in the correct manner. This is a win-win situation for you each time.

How to handle Voicemails

A majority of people read voice messages and take in the information. They don't bother to keep track of the information, believing that since it's stored, it will be available whenever they require it. However, voice messages are not as reliable as information that can be incorporated into an organization system. Most of the time, voice messages will be deleted, or the individual forgets where the information is. When you write down information it is more real because you've experienced the details personally, and you've got the information in tangible form.

Voicemails should be treated as you would phone calls. Record who the call came from, what the phone call was about and your contact details when applicable. Sometimes, voicemails are simply reminders to contact a person back . You can then enter the information in the "To-Do" list, under calls you need to make. Sometimes, a voicemail is a request to forward information, but this time ensure that you record the information into your organization system to be processed. At a minimum, you must record the individual's contact details and add the information to your system database.

Handling Texts

Text messages are an excellent option to stay in touch when you're traveling or you are unable to reach reception to make a phone call. As technology improves, we'll have different options to texting. It is essential to treat text messages for work just as any other type of information. Schedule time each day to make sure you've recorded the text messages you receive into your organization system. Record important information and store them in the correct spot.

Text messages usually need more details, so before acting, make use of the messages to start the process. It is possible to have the area designated for messages sent via text. If you record the details, you can put them into the box or file and then take action when the moment is right. Do not assume the fact that you have the data since it's recorded as text on your phone. It's possible to lose the phone, delete it accidentally, text, or simply not have it in your pocket when you need this information. For example, you might be talking with someone on the phone and require details from the text. It's difficult to extract that information from your text while talking on the phone. You could even be disconnected. If, however, you've logged the data in a safe location which you can access quickly and easily, you'll be better on your way. Additionally in incorporating text-related information in your plan of action and schedule, you'll not be thrown off-track when work-related messages come in. Even if you do not text frequently, by planning for it now, you'll be prepared if in the near future, you decide to write more frequently as part of your job.

Controlling Instant Messaging, Social Networking , and Personal calls

In the end, it is important to take instant messages as an incoming telephone call, voice mail or text. Transform the information you need into a format that fits in your personal design to ensure that it is available at the time you require it.

The main issue with instant messaging is that it could interrupt your workflow and interrupt your energy levels. Although technology has made communication with people easy however, there are some occasions when you must be unavailable due to doing a lot of work. Instant messaging is perfect when you want an immediate response to a colleague but not when you're working and your you want to talk with a friend.

Similar to social media sites like Facebook or Twitter can mess up your routine and destroy your system of organization. The interruption of personal calls can ruin your schedule and prevent you from completing your work however, you do not want to appear rude or unfriendly. How do you handle these interruptions and not let them consume your day? Let's take a look at ways you can keep your social requirements met while working.

The first is that most instant messaging websites allow you to control whether you're available for chat with other users or not. If you regularly use apps that let you chat on the internet, you can go to the settings and toggle off your availability. It is possible to switch it on when you're in a hurry however, leaving it open all day is a great way to be tempted. If you receive an instant message, it may be difficult to ignore. A coworker or friend might believe that you're unprofessional if you don't reply and, before you know it, you've spent an entire hour talking when you should be doing something productive. However, if you're not around then they will not bother them in the first instance. Set a specific time of the week or day where online chat is permitted. Make sure that you're not violating any company guidelines by communicating on the internet. That way, when you do engage in chat, you'll be able to be sure that you are doing it in a safe manner.

Social media sites offer another major draw. A lot of people prefer to go through their Facebook or news feed each when they log on to the internet. It's true that there's something wrong with the social network. However, it must be handled efficiently. Schedule time for checking and updating your website. Utilize social media time to reward yourself for completing undesirable tasks. Make sure that you don't permit yourself to spend longer using these websites than you have planned. Change the settings to ensure that they do not open on a regular basis or alert you each when someone sends you an email. You should ensure that you appear with the label "offline" even when you're closing the page running as a background on your laptop. In this way, you'll be able to be able to manage social media accounts in an efficient manner that is acceptable for bosses.

In the end text messages and calls to family members aren't always easy, particularly in the case of friends and relatives who do not respect your working hours. When you're working, you should limit your personal calls. It is best to turn your ringer off and make your family and friends be aware that you can only be reached in situation in the event of an emergency. Many times when you progress in your profession and your personal availability for calls will shift. What was considered acceptable last year might not be the same this year. Make sure you communicate with the people you love to ensure they know your goals and the reasons the reasons why your work environment is changing. Schedule time in your schedule to look over your phone to see if you missed calls, voicemailmessages, and texts. There's nothing wrong with receiving messages, provided you don't allow them to disrupt your day. Your cell phone could be an integral element of your organization's design however, you must be in control of it. Don't let your career be lost due to unwelcome and inconvenient phone calls.

Chapter 8: Tips To Make Your System Flexible To Career Advancement

The last aspect of the success of an organizational system is being flexible. The most serious flaw in an organizational structure occurs when the design is too rigid or it becomes more crucial to keep the system running rather than getting the job completed. The world never stays the same. If it's a shift in your job, technological advancements or the necessity for someone else to take over your job in order to give you your much-needed time off, your organizational system has to be able evolve and change to keep up with the demands of your profession.

You can take a few hours and design a new system, but the true value of an organized system is that even minor adjustments are able to ensure that you are working at your the highest level. Be aware that the system needs to be adapted to your needs and not just your job and therefore the basic elements will remain the same unless there is a significant shift. For example, you could make a career change and enter an entirely new field however, you're still exactly the same. If you enjoy the order of things and work using tangible objects rather than having everything done on a computer These aspects will not change , and your organization's design must reflect this.

What we need to accomplish is to identify the elements that could change and those that aren't. It's fairly easy. What aspects that you have in your computer are essential to you? In terms of your favorite parts and appreciate the most that you would never ever For example, for certain people using their online schedules is essential to them. If you are a tech enthusiast and appreciate the possibility of having a calendar that can keep up with your needs regardless of what device you're using, the feature should not alter. However it is possible that you be working with lots of hard copies and file them in filing cabinets and you'll be less concerned about working with digital or hard copy files. It's possible that this will change, and you're aware that you could make changes if required. The last thing you wish to do is alter those aspects that matter to you.

Making adjustments to meet new Responsibilities

As you increase your performance, don't be shocked when your bosses start to observe that you are improving. Even if you're not the best performer in your field you should see an immense difference in what you can accomplish when you have an efficient system for organizing. If you're not able to do more work in less time, then you should take a close review of your organization. Is it as easy as you can make it? Are you taking a long time using on the system? Do you have trouble managing your tasks and people, information & Time? These are indicators that something is wrong with the way you design. It could also be because you're not using your daily energy flow or managing time as you ought to However, most of the time you will notice the difference. As people walk by your workplace, they'll be amazed by how neat and tidy your workspace is. When they notice your work, it won't take long before you have new tasks coming your way. They will start to view you as someone who is able to complete work effectively, or who is able to take on important jobs. I hope that all of this leads to advancement in your career and your organization skills will develop with you.

If you've been given new responsibilities, you should take some time to consider your organization system. Do you need to make changes? Are you able to incorporate the new tasks into your existing process? Sometimes, just by creating new priorities, you'll be able to incorporate new tasks. If you are offered a new position or change in your job position, then you could need to reconsider your entire method of working. Consider how the you will be able to manage the tasks that come through your work space. Perhaps you're in a new position where everything is digital, and your entry point must be a particular area in your laptop. Perhaps you have to adapt to supervising others. Perhaps your duties aren't just documents however, they are the people who work on the files. If you're facing a major shift in the work that you are responsible for, you'll need to incorporate the previous methods used prior to the change and adjust it to your new role. Perhaps you've experienced the biggest shift in the past by staying on top of the essential tasks and making sure that they were completed in a timely manner. Now, you must train your entire team or department to operate in the same manner. You'll have to spend some time with the new people and prioritize your tasks so that you are able to achieve results quickly and make the most impression in your new job.

The most important thing is to hang the procedures loosely. You'll want to carry on your current procedures, but the procedures that worked in your previous job may not be effective once you are given new tasks. Many people struggle to make their previous organization design work for their new job. They are the ones who are unhappy with their work , and aren't able to move forward or being eventually let go. You must be able to implement changes as they become necessary and recognize the key elements that help your organization suitable for your needs. With this information you'll be able to perform in any circumstance.

Working Offsite

One of the most difficult problems for individuals are when new duties require them to work outside of the office. If you're used to spending all of your working hours at the workplace, with your design for organization easily set up and ready to access You'll have to adjust quickly. If you're promoted and are forced travel frequently, then how can you adjust your system of organization to accommodate being away from your desk? Let's examine three principles to help you stay in order if you must travel away from your normal workplace on a frequent basis.

First, go mobile. It is essential to transfer the majority of your data as you can to mobile devices. You might have already accomplished this, but if are planning to travel, it's essential. I also recommend you to setup online storage of your files to ensure that you are able to access your files at any time and wherever. When you are mobile, it is important to ensure that your devices are connected and share data with the smallest of steps. It's not unusual for things to change while out in the field, as you'd prefer not to miss some important information since it was updated via your mobile device but not your main workstation. The worst part is the constant updating of each device one at moment, after the change has been implemented. Take care of your own so that the pressure of working in a different regular routine and making adjustments to your system of organization doesn't take too much of your time.

And, thirdly Importantly take time each week to consider your organization's design. If it's making a list of your current tasks or working through projects that were accumulated during the time you were absent, it can keep you sane. If you don't schedule the time then you'll find yourself tempted to be busy right away and your system of organization is likely to fall apart. If you're traveling, your system of organization is more vital than ever so make time (even only 15 minutes per week) to change your strategy to your strategies, adjust approaches and prioritize. You'll be amazed at what time and energy you could save by spending just a few minutes at the start of every week preparing.

In the end, you must alter your perception. It's true that working offsite will be in several ways different than working in your regular work environment, but if you are able to change your mindset, you'll realize that working off site is just another thing to do. Make a notepad to place into your work folder that lists what you have to complete each time you're off-site. Most likely, you'll be given some notice in the form of an "task" for each visit it will be easier to organize it in your plan with only minor adjustments. There will certainly be tasks that are specifically being carried out that must be categorized under subcategories within your system of organization however the most important thing is to not overlook the benefits you've gained from organizing. This particular task requires you to be not only from your work space however, but also away from your office entirely. It's fine, just save what you're working on prior to leaving in the unfinished file and complete the task when you return. It is your goal to keep your tasks in order and in order; therefore, do not let time slip away and distract you from your goals.

Planning for time away from work

We've discussed working off-site however, what happens the times when you're away for vacation, sick leave, or pregnant leave? What should your system of organization adjust for these periods? In the first place, it should be easy for your coworkers to find what they need within your office without having to pester you. The last thing you want during your trip is answering calls from colleagues who require information from you that they cannot locate. If your system is self-explanatory or extremely individualized, before you leave , take five minutes to train at least one of your coworkers on the way your system operates to ensure they find what they need , and also help others find the information they need. If you do an excellent job of explaining the system you'll be less stressed and, hopefully, your workplace will not be in a mess when you return after a day of those who are in search of what they require.

Also, create a space where you can work in. Do not expect others to know where you are for work currently in progress. Place a bin in the corner with a clearly marked label, so that those who leave your job will know where to put it. There may be a lot of things to sort through before returning at work. However, with this method there will be no misplaced items and your office isn't cluttered by hard copies of work that must be completed. A tidy and organized file will allow you to return at work in a positive attitude, and also accomplish tasks in a timely manner so that your work does not get slowed down.

Transferring Your System's Information

Another advantage of having a well-organized system is that if you're promoted or moved out of the position it is possible to transfer the system to another person. One of the greatest obstacles to being promoted is the effort that it requires to replace the person who replaced you. In the event that you've got an procedure in place that you are able to transfer your knowledge to the new person, it will make you a top potential candidate for promotion. You can offer to guide your new employee or assist others to take on your clients and see the same results you enjoyed. Of course, the method will have to be adapted to suit the new person Don't be inflexible about them performing the same thing as you did. It is important to emphasize the things that worked for you and the reason for that. If someone is intelligent, they'll implement a lot of what you have designed however ultimately it is entirely up to them. Your aim should be to help educate them and then take your organization abilities to the next step.

If you're organized You'll not only be able to keep on top of your workload with greater efficiency and you'll also appreciate your work more as well as receive greater recognition and benefits, and advance your career. This is an enormous advantage for you since you don't have to learn the wrong system that might not be appropriate for your current job. Instead, you've learned to develop an organization system that works for you. You can tweak it, tweak it , and completely alter it if needed. Have fun and remember that everyone can get organized. What are you waiting for? Get organized!

Chapter 9: Organizing Your Basement, Storage Spaces And Attics

This chapter is going be about organizing other spaces leftover within your home, such as basements, attics storage spaces, and basement. These are the areas of your home that tend to hold whatever you can't fit elsewhere and will likely require the most time to arrange.

In order to begin organizing the areas you're in, you'll be required to sit down and look through all the belongings and determine what you'd like to save and which are able to live with. There are bound to be several things in these rooms of your house you've put off throughout the years, and has no use any more. Make the effort to eliminate everything haven't been used for many years and don't have any use anymore. You may be amazed at the amount of space you'll have left in these spaces and how much task will be reduced.

After you have finished deciding what you'd like to keep and which you'll be throwing to the curb There are a few actions you can take to sort out those things that you have left over. It is important to decide, from the items you have left to decide which items you are likely to be using frequently and which you require every once in a once in a while. For instance, if are storing cleaning materials in a closet for storage then you'll want them located in front of them to make it easy to get there easily. Things like Christmas decorations would be suitable to the rear of the storage space.

It is also advisable to be thinking about your storage vertically. your storage spaces. If there's shelving , make sure you take advantage of it and arrange everything you can in an orderly way. If your room doesn't contain any shelves it is possible to think about adding some shelves to the space. It is an easy method of getting things out away from view and make it easier to organize an area that can be very messy. These shelves are an ideal way to categorize items that have a similar design and allows you to find the items you have stored in the storage space.

Then, you'll need take into consideration the potential hazards associated with certain items particularly in the context of storing items in your attics and basements. If you've got lots of valuables you keep in the basement, ensure that they are kept off the ground so that they don't become vulnerable to damage from water. The items that are stored in the attic must be able to withstand extreme fluctuations in temperature so you need to be cautious about what you store in this location.

Clear containers are your most trusted companion for these storage spaces. You can put tons of stuff in these bins, and you can determine what's inside each one with small effort. Be cautious about the size of bins you buy. Although it may seem like an ideal idea to buy large bins to store many things however, it'll soon become too heavy to move. Choose smaller bins that are able to hold a few items inside for ease of movement and accessibility.

One thing you must remember when you organize the storage spaces in your house is that you do not have to use an emergency flashlight to determine what's where. If you're making use of a flashlight each whenever you enter any of the storage spaces it is likely that you have not properly organized the space. Include some lighting to these areas and arrange things in order so that when you step to the storage area you can know what's in the area easily without using the need for a flashlight.

Labeling is a must when organizing the storage spaces within your home. Whatever you decide to do it is impossible to recall the contents of each bin for a few months later. Create notes or labelers to indicate what's in each bin while you go through the process.

It is also important to to organize the storage spaces a priority to make sure they don't get messy and unorganized again. It is recommended that you make this a priority at least once or two every year. It is often easy to dump things in storage spaces, and you'll soon be in a mess. A every year to clean it up will make the chore easier to manage and will help you to to track the items you keep in your storage room.

Chapter 10: Maintaining Your Organization

Once you've spent the time to follow the suggestions listed in this book on how to manage your home, it's time to think of ways to maintain your organization instead of reverting to your old routines and seeing your home turn into a mess just a few months after. This chapter is dedicated to providing you with a few easy guidelines to use to keep your home's organization in the long-term.

First of all first, you must ensure you feel that your experience of organizing will make you feel happy. If you are happy with the effort you put into organizing, you'll be more likely to do it later on. Furthermore that, once you've spent the time to locate the right place for all the things that you have in your home, it's essential to do it each day. After you have finished using the item, you should put it away promptly to keep it out of the way. A few more suggestions on how could be done to ensure the order of your home include:

1. Regular maintenance: Instead of waiting for your home's condition to turn an absolute mess and then having to clean it up, spend just a few minutes each day to perform an easy clean.

2. Take note of this: as you're doing those couple of minutes of cleaning every day, take some moment to reflect on the kinds of organization that are effective and which you aren't fond of. Write down the things you dislike to be able to use them next time you need to do the complete cleaning of your home.

3. Re-organize Your home: Whatever effort you do to organize your home on a daily basis There will come an time when clutter will begin to return. If this is frequent, you may be required to take some time to think of an alternative method of organizing that is better for your requirements.

4. If it's working, do not waste your time on it. It doesn't make sense to spend lots hours trying to repair systems that are

functioning perfectly for you. Fix only the systems of organization that cause you problems.

5. Be grateful for the work you're doing. You've spent a lot of time and effort into your home, so it is essential to stop and take note of it. If you enjoy the place that you live living in, you'll be inclined to care for it better.

6. You can earn an incentive for keeping your home neat If you make organizing into something that is a chore, you're more likely to not keep going. Instead, transform it into an activity you appreciate and then add an incentive to keep it going and you'll be more likely to continue organizing.

There are other considerations you should be aware of when you're trying to organize your home. The first is to remember that things don't have to be perfect when you're organizing your first time. Find a method that is most effective for you now. And should it not working in the future you are able to alter the system.

Even if you don't have much funds to get organized in your home doesn't suggest that you are unable to come up with some innovative ways to organize your home. The ability to think creatively is among the most valuable skills you can use if you're in a tight budget.

It is also possible to realize that investing a small amount of money to organize your home can be a worthwhile investment in the future. Containers for organization like key racks, shelf racks, and various containers can be able to pay for themselves in terms of comfort within a few months. If you're worried about finances, you'll have the option of using one or two of the containers, or other objects in your house instead of buying new things.

The main thing you need to keep in mind about the process of organizing is to organize it in a manner that is most beneficial for you. The method that is effective for one person may turn disastrously for you. Make sure to begin your organization process by going through the room and getting rid of things you no longer need. This will help you save a lot of time and effort once you're ready to arrange the remainder of your room.

Chapter 11: General Tips

First, make lists of everything. The brain is designed to be creators that come up with new concepts and ideas frequently. They're not designed to hold large amounts of information. If you're filling up the space inside your brain with data that doesn't have to be stored there, you're hindering your capacity to think and develop thoughts. Instead, make lists that contain relevant information. Noting down information and getting the information out of your mind is not just a way to organize them but also allows you to make the brain space so that it can perform the task it is designed to do. This helps that you keep the thoughts organized.

Writing lists allows you to organize relevant information into groups and speed the process of retrieving this information later. Let's look at the buying list to give an illustration. It's not necessary to remember particular items. When you are thinking of something you'd like to purchase put it on your list of shopping. If you need to know which foods to purchase for your next trip, like when you're heading to the local store You can look over your list of items and view all the details in one spot at a glance. A shopping list lets you batch your purchases. Instead of visiting the store several times per week to pick up a few of things, you can combine your food items and purchase everything at once, which will save time.

Writing lists lets you ensure that all pertinent and related information is stored in one place. Examples of lists you can keep are:

Groceries

Chores

Birthdays

Upcoming events

To-Do Lists

DIY-related activities

Emails to respond to

Books to be read

Films to be able to

The next step is a good follow-up which is to write or write down everything. Like the reasons of making lists, by writing everything off your mind and onto paper or in a virtual document, you clear space in your brain and let your brain do what it is best at create thoughts. This helps save brain power also, which allows you to focus on other important tasks. Lists are helpful for keeping important information in one place. writing down everything down is helpful to ensure optimal brain function.

A great tip for organisation is to create a plan and plan ahead for everything. If you're planning on undertaking something in the near future, make plans in advance and plan the things you'll need to be brought along. Even for smaller things like going to town taking a backpack with you and taking all the things you'll require - along with other items like an water bottle or small journals - could help if an occasion occurs. It's possible that you'll be out longer than you expected and be unable to purchase a drink, or you may encounter someone who has incredibly valuable details to record.

Making plans in advance can reduce stress and stress, and keep you relaxed at ease, confident, and well-informed on your trip. It's not about scheduling the entire hour, minute or minute of your activities. Simply check the essentials like what the weather is likely to be like, the public transportation or fuel stations as well as what type of clothing you'll need or may require or require, etc. This will help you maintain security and help ensure that you get the most of each excursion and activity.

The next two suggestions are for physical items , and will make your life easier and save space. First, you should stop having cash in your purse or wallet. It's not necessary. We live in a digital world that allows you to utilize cards for a lot of things. The best option is to have an only card wallet since it will save space. Notes are more suitable since they fold but they aren't necessary. There's a possible exception to this, and that is to keep some coins of the pound in your bag or backpack for the occasion that you need them in the event of a need.

Then, separate your keys according to their purpose and identify them accordingly. This will help you recognize which key belongs to the lock you want to unlock, and saves time since you don't need to look up every key each time you need to open some thing. A small, sticky notepad will do the trick as will a keyring that works equally useful. It is possible to take it an extra step by separating keys that are frequently used in conjunction, for instance with car and home keys, garage and shed keys key for the back door and shed.

The next tip general is important every day - plan your outfit for the next day at night. This means you don't have to decide at the beginning of the day, conserving your willpower for later decisions. It also allows you get to work or where you're going in a shorter time.

The creation of a physical box

Your work environment and life style will affect the amount of documents, receipts, letters and files you've at any point. The more physical documents you own and the more you'll gain from this idea: creating a physical mailbox. In essence, it's the place you put every single physical document and you can sort through them every week, ideally on the day you have designated for your organisation (Sunday). Anything that is paper-based will go in this inbox.

When you go through the files, you can sort them into three methods:

Take a picture or scan (or take a picture) digitally, and then save on your personal computer or in the Cloud. Recycle or trash the image.

Sort the file into a physical folder. Most often, this is done for important documents you need an actual copy of - for example, birth certificates or a university degrees. It's also worth purchasing a physical folder to store these kinds of documents instead of putting them in a paper box or plastic pocket.

Recycle or Bin

Every file should be sorted into one of three methods. If you don't need the physical copy and will require the data in the future then scan it. If you're required to keep an actual copy, store the file in an physical folder. Otherwise, you can reuse the document.

Any file that doesn't require the physical copy of the file and isn't in use can be saved and scanned. If you're uncertain about a file and it doesn't need your immediate attention, you can put it back in your email to review the next week. A fresh outlook can be helpful.

Receipts, specifically, can be photographed or scanned and saved in an appropriate directory on your PC. In this case it is recommended to label them with a date , along with the item purchased. If you're not likely to require the receipt, for instance to shop for your weekly groceries you can keep it without scanning.

More General Tips

This leads nicely to our next point Do not let things pile up. Paper pieces and books, dishes that are dirty, and even old clothes are an example of what may quickly pile up if not properly managed. If you notice things beginning to pile up, you must act immediately . Perform the appropriate actions and then put everything back in its proper location.

Making sure that everything has a place "live" is extremely beneficial for organization. What I am referring to is to dedicate each item in your home to a particular spot, in which it will remain until used. There are two advantages to this practice that you can see: first, you will are aware of where an item is when you require it, reducing the time of searching for it. Furthermore, it keeps things tidy, organized, and manageable. Instead of asking yourself 'where should I store this?' and then throwing it into a drawer, give the item an area where it can be. Of course, you are able to move these places around however the idea is identical. When you do this, you will also add the control aspect into your life.

One thing that can greatly assist with this last suggestion is to invest on an EDC tray -

also known as an Everyday C tray for your jewellery. It's a small tray you can buy at a reasonable price, and where you can store things like your phone, wallet keys, a pen headphones, coins and other jewellery. A good EDC tray can help you find things you use frequently and will prevent the loss of essential items such as your keys.

Journaling

There are many tips to keeping a journal and having journals, which is why I've put them all together in this section.

The first step is to actually start journaling. This could be regular journals or using bullets. Make sure to keep all of your notes and writing in one location in your journal. Also, note down your writing regularly, marking the relevant dates. This is particularly helpful to write lists or general notes. With all your writing information stored in one place your organization can be improved. If you need to locate something was written in the past then you can refer to the journal rather than scouring through multiple pieces of paper.

When you add a title as well as an entry's date This will make your journal easier to read. It is also helpful to label each page with a number and then make the table of contents at the beginning of your journal, with appropriate pages and titles. In the event that your journals are mostly regular or everyday entries you could put the title in a grouping such as Daily entries from May 1st through May 31st page 41'.

If you want to learn more about bullet journaling specifically, you can head to https://bulletjournal.com/ or search 'bullet journal' on YouTube to receive thousands of useful results. I've recently implemented in my life and have seen my productivity and organisation improve substantially.

Another suggestion for organizing is to keep a notebook or notepad wherever you travel. Even if it's an A5-sized or A6 notepad, simply by having something you can write on, you'll gain a lot. Thoughts, ideas and ideas can spring up from all sorts of places , and being able to capture these thoughts makes sure you don't forget these ideas.

The best plans for life and business come from the most ordinary scenarios. If you don't have a notebook to record these thoughts in, you'll probably lose them, and miss great opportunities.

Additionally you could find that your laptop or mobile might fail and you may require an area to note something down like directions. Another scenario that could happen is that you could meet a beautiful woman or guy who gives you their number. If you don't have a notepad it is possible to lose out on a potential love interest! You'll be thankful when you get there.

Belongings

It's normal that as humans that we'll gather a lot of "stuff throughout the course of time and over the years. It's a good thing you have systems in place and follow these tips to control the clutter.

The most significant lifestyle change that can assist you in managing your belongings is becoming minimalist. It is a good idea to take a look at what minimalism means and then adapt some of the rules and methods that come from it. It is not necessary to adhere to absurd rules like owning 100 or less items instead, think about adopting an approach that is minimalist to your possessions.

The next step is to think about getting rid of your old possessions. There's no need for random toys from your childhood or old T-shirts. Shot glasses and wristbands from the university may also go. The storage of old things that have little or no purpose can consume space both physically and mentally. It's a simple rule that can be extremely helpful in determining how much clutter you have in your home - one in and one out. In essence, each time you're planning to buy an item that is new must remove items that you have already used.
If you're planning to adhere to this policy, ensure that all items fall within the same category, for example, kitchen appliances, or toys. It's not worth getting rid of a sock

that's been used if you're looking to buy an updated TV as they're not suited to the same purposes.

I love applying this rule for clothing specifically. If you're looking to purchase an entirely new t-shirt, it is first necessary to sell, give away, or dispose of an old T-shirt. This will ensure that you don't overdo it with clothes to wear, and also keeps your wardrobe clean.

You should consider investing in storage bins. If you intend to keep lots of stuff, it'll be beneficial to have a designated space for storing that stuff. You can organize items and place them in storage bins like shoes, toys and tools as well as equipment for hobbies can be stored in the appropriate storage bins. The shelves can also work however they don't hold the same amount of. This is a tip to give each item its own space, but goes further by putting items in groups. Toiletries, stationery books, technology items are a few more examples of things that are able to be put in shelves or bins.

Scheduling

One of the most popular strategy for managing time is scheduling. It is the ultimate example of efficient time management; it's used to manage your time instead of your daily activities and possessions. Your schedule does not have to be fixed in blocks, nor does every minute of your day have to be scheduled out. I personally like flexibility in my schedule where I set each day a primary goal and a set of work tasks and let the hours take care of by themselves. It is difficult for me to adhere to a strict timetable, and this is the way that works best for me.

You could be able to benefit from a more strict and more structured schedule. you'll need to test to determine for sure.

At first choose the method of creating your schedule . It can be digital or written. I prefer digital, using Google Calendar. You can use a whiteboard, journal or a plain piece of paper could be a good idea. But the benefit of using a digital calendar is that it can be accessed via the internet from wherever you are. It isn't necessary to carry the white paper, or even a huge piece of whiteboard everywhere you travel.

An excellent place to begin is to provide each day with an agenda and activities and I'm not declaring that because that's my job. We already have a day devoted to chores and organization Let's not forget Sundays to show an for an example. On Sundays I complete the tasks unfinished in the week, and spend the rest of the day free.

There are six additional days with tasks to complete. It's great for our mental health and well-being to have a few days off every week. I have found it best to take Saturday off. ideal day to do this. So, we have the typical 5-day working week. Your job duties will be different from mine, but I'll give you my current schedule so that you can get an understanding of how to schedule your own.

Writing and YouTube videos on Monday.

Tuesday Blog post transcription and light writing/planning

Wednesday Writing ebook content, business management Research

Thursday - A detailed blog post writing

Video on Friday writing, finishing weekly chores

Every day isn't limited to these specific activities, however I strive to adhere to the above-mentioned schedule. I plan my day in the morning , and plan other one-off tasks after I've completed the above repeated actions.

Once you've got an overall understanding of what you need to complete on which days, you can start making time slots and arranging the priority of completion. The most important tasks must be completed first and at a time when you are most efficient. For me, this is the morning. Based on how strict your schedule is you'll need to calculate the amount of time the task itself will last.

To assist in understanding the duration of your work and your most productive times of the day, record your work time and activities throughout the week. It's not necessary to record every minute, but intervals of 15 or 30 minutes are better. Pay attention to the time frame in which you are most productive.

What is the length you would like your working days to last? 8 hours could be required by your work, therefore you'll need to set aside the time you'll need for working. If you work at home or have a self-employed job you'll have more control over the amount and the time you work. Instead of a single block, you could plan four 2-hour blocks that are scheduled at various times during the day. The way you approach it will affect the schedule you have.

Then, you can schedule the times to repeat your activities. For instance, you could join a club for hobbies each week, or go to an exercise class each Thursday in the morning. You can incorporate this into your routine.

If you regularly exercise but do not adhere following a strict routine take time to block portions of time that you can roughly adhere to. I work out in the morning, between 8 until 10 am on

Wednesdays, Mondays and on Fridays. Additionally, I exercise on other days, with Saturday being the exception and Sunday, which lasts for about 30 minutes between 8AM and 8:30 AM.

I would strongly suggest to set a waking time and get up every day at the same time. This will not only help your circadian rhythm, which will allow you to sleep and rise earlier as well, it can also help your schedule and weekly structure. When you wake up every day at the exact time each throughout the day, you'll find your routine will become more stable and less likely to be thrown off.

The evenings are free of any structure, or designated as free time. You can use this time as you'd would like. It is helpful to establish a time when you will get ready to go to your bed. This is a great idea when you set a time for waking up; this will make sure you get at least 7 and one-half hours of rest every night.

Approach your schedule however you like. You can draft an outline of your plan, like making use of one-hour chunks (look at time-blocking) or scheduling activities every 15 minutes. No matter what method you pick make sure you have an organized schedule will bring more order and organization to your life.

Weekly activities

To conclude this section, here are some suggestions for activities you can perform once a week on your designated time for organization or a day to do chores. These activities will improve the organization in your life:

A quick cleaning of your home
Make sure your home is tidy
Washing clothes
Cleaning bathrooms
The week's plans for the coming week
Changing bedding
Preparing meals
The week's budgeting process to come
Controlling your the inbox of your email
Controlling your physical inbox
The week's goals should be set for the coming week
Work schedule for the coming week
Creating your weekly schedule

Organising digital environment
Electronics that charge
Grooming
Chatting with a loved one
Tidying your desk space
The Most Important Tips
First and foremost, you must choose an organizational strategy and method that works for you . Get ideas and inspiration from each of these ideas along with the other digital suggestions, and create your own system. You'll be the one who will be the main user of your system, therefore design an item that is optimized for your personal lifestyle.

Perhaps you aren't a fan of extreme organization, preferring more freedom and flexibility. This is fine However, when you're reading this article, I'd suppose that you have at the very least some desire to become more organized. If you prefer to be less organized, set up some routines and systems in place to make sure that things don't get excessively out of control. Cleaning and organizing each week is an excellent starting point. Once you've done that, you'll be able to pick any of the daily activities listed above.

Digital Management and Digitisation
In the last 20 years, we've witnessed the largest shift in human history, principally because of the broad use and availability of technology. One of the greatest advantages that this has brought is the capacity to utilize digital technology instead of the traditional ways of writing. Today, it's more popular to write on the laptop or computer instead of pencil and paper. Technology is easier to use today and work access is readily and instantly accessible because of the Cloud which allows us to save our work online and retrieve it from another location with no loss of data. Incredible.
Another advantage can be that storage that is digital consumes significantly less physical space than traditional methods. A 2 Terabyte (2000gb of information) external hard drive can be considerably smaller than a physical 200-page folder. The result for us in terms of organisation is

that we can save your files electronically and save space, but also adds more organization for our daily lives. It's much easier to search through and find files within an online directory than to browse through a file cabinet. Thanks for the search feature!

It's not a problem, physical files still have value and have a function, but for everyday organization, digitizing your files can be a game changer. This chapter will provide suggestions for digitizing your files and organizing and managing your technology systems.

The Digitisation Rule

To ensure optimal organization it is recommended to follow the "digitisation rule" In other words, if it's digitally recorded or accessed electronically but doesn't take up physical space.

Two major advantages of this rule have recently been discussed the instant accessibility from any place and the reduction of physical space. In light of this, it's no longer necessary to maintain physical copies of almost everything.

DVDs are now practically non-existent thanks the advent of Netflix and other streaming services.

Music albums have been evolving backwards old-fashioned vinyl CDs are becoming more popular and trendy and Spotify and SoundCloud allow music listening quick, easy and available any time.

Video Games are now available as digital downloads that take up the physical space instead of the physical space.

When was the last time that you snapped a polaroid photo?

In the end, due to the wide usage of these tools that we do not have to store things physically. It is a vast array of different services that help us run our modern society that having physical space is inefficient.

There are of course certain exceptions to this policy. There are times when you need to keep items in physical form to preserve sentimental value, or simply for the sake of having the physical copy. It's nice to have an actual copy of your favorite film on DVD, however having a collection of more than 200 old films would be a waste of space. Many streaming services offer an array of content to pick from that almost the majority of your 200-year-old films are available on the internet. You can write an inventory of those 200+ films using Google Docs and save the list in digital format, allowing you to recall the DVDs you've bought over your lifetime. However, if you weren't interested in streaming service, you can buy an external HDD to store the films on it in digital format.

Digital File Management

There's a certain amount of satisfaction when having all your digital files properly organized. The proper structure of your files established, moving files off of your desktop and using appropriate name conventions are just a few of the basic benefits of digital organization. This not only speeds up your workflow, it also lets you find more quickly by using a simpler organized navigation.

Before we start discussing the management of digital files is to mention how your files are bound to be messy. For me I'm talking about the downloads folder, which can quickly accumulate. In no time there will be hundreds of files to go through, and it gets more difficult as I let it sit. To aid in this you can put in place specific systems, routines and routines to make sure your digital world stays tidy and clean.

The first approach is identical to our chores day from chapter 1. every week, go through and arrange the digital data you have. In reality, it's better to complete this task on the same day you complete everything else, because of the benefits of batching as well as the increased organization. The process of sorting digital files isn't any time at all, so by committing 15 minutes every week to put things back in order you'll be able to create more peace in your life and be able to keep a productive workflow.

It is also possible to create your own habit by sorting the files according to how you see them on your PC. Each time you download something via the internet, you should move it from your download folder to the appropriate directory. In addition, start saving files to your downloads folder rather than your desktop. That's what is it for. Create folders specific to every work project and save files relevant to them, instead of the general 'work' folder or, even worse it's the default document folder.

Naming Conventions

Does it bother me that this sort of stuff makes me happy? Probably. However they are, naming conventions are one of the primary aspects that assist with digital organization. It's important to think about this prior to the file structure is created since naming conventions aid in understanding details in the future.

What are the naming conventions? They are basically ways to name your digital files so that they're properly listed and are easy to use. If someone who isn't familiar with your system isn't able to make use of it, then the system is too complex. Fortunately, the system of naming conventions I'm about to show you is extremely easy to use.

In the beginning, you should avoid spaces, especially in the event that you are planning to use this file for online use. From the perspective of a programmer the use of spaces in filenames is an issue. Have you ever opened a PDF or file in your web browser that has spaces in its name, and the file name looks like 'This%20is%20a%PDF%20file '? Spaces in the file name, are replaced by the number %20. This is a problem when typing out and moving through command prompts or hosting, since every time you encounter a space , you need to substitute %20. Instead using underscores , '_' or '"-" as opposed to spaces. I use underscores in general usage and use dashes to indicate tags. These will be the topics I'll be talking about later.

To aid in reading to make reading easier, you can employ the system of naming known as Pascal Case - in essence it is the capitalization of every letter in each word. This is especially important in the absence of spaces since it can be extremely difficult to identify what word is which. Additionally, file names could contain offensive words that aren't something you want to see in the files you share to your employer. Let me offer an example to clarify the issue.

No spaces: animalstudyswanalpaca
Spaces: Animal Study Swan alpaca
Pascal Case: AnimalStudySwanAlpaca

Even though the name isn't the most appealing (I'd call it Something like Study-AlpacaSwan) You should know the concept. If you don't use Pascal Case, file names are often messy and difficult to comprehend. It is possible to use underscores to separate words If you'd like this, which is the default option I use when the filename is comprised of several words that are easily divided.

For example, under this system, the May Finance Report' might change to:
MayFinanceReport
May_FinanceReport
May_Finance_Report

Personally, out of three options, I'd go to the third choice. Another method of name files is to use dashes. I like using dashes especially for what I refer to as 'tags that are descriptive words that can help differentiate an individual file from the rest. For instance, suppose you have financial reports for the first quarter of this year. It makes sense to me, to rename these documents:

FinanceReport-Jan

FinanceReport-Feb

FinanceReport-Mar

If you sort by alphabet then you'll be putting all financial reports together. But even though they're grouped together, it doesn't mean they'll be chronologically ordered or in the order you want them to be. This is why we are starting by using numbers.

One of the advantages of using numbers to name files is that the number 0 is followed by one and then 2, and then 3, etc. - which allows you to identify files with numbers and alter the order to suit your preferences. If the beginning of a filename appears repeatedly, as in the case of FinanceReport it will scan every character and look for the alphabet (or numbers) that doesn't repeat and will sort the file alphabetically. FinanceReport-Feb will sort prior to FinanceReport-Jan in alphabetical order, but it wouldn't show chronologically.

Instead it is possible to make numbers on the filename, which we can list in a customized order:

FinanceReport01-Jan

FinanceReport02-Feb

FinanceReport03-Mar

If we now sort alphabetically, we'll do it in the proper order.

An important note: if you do not include a zero before the selected number or two zeros when you have many files, they could appear in an unintentional order. The system will scan each character the character, therefore FinanceReport11 will sort prior to FinanceReport2, whereas FinanceReport11 will sort following FinanceReport02.

Similar to triple digits. FinanceReport100 will sort out after FinanceReport2 100 will sort in the same way as the number 002.

What happens do you do if you have financial statements for several years? It is possible to sort them according to the chronological system above and it would be a good idea and I'd suggest. You can also think of naming something like this, which will sort alphabetically in this manner:

FinanceReport01-Jan2020
FinanceReport01-Jan2021
FinanceReport02-Feb2020
FinanceReport02-Feb2021

However, the issue is that you may want reports to be grouped by year. In this scenario you'd have to record the year prior to the month's start date, so it's like:

FinanceReport2020-01Jan
FinanceReport2020-02Feb
FinanceReport2021-01Jan
FinanceReport2021-02Feb

It is generally recommended to place numbers at the beginning of the filename, or prior to the relevant words. The numbers will always appear ahead of alphabetically listed letters, therefore, by doing this, you can be sure that your files are displayed in the order you prefer. It is also possible to use 000 at the beginning of the filename to place your file towards the highest within your folder (alphabetically).

It is also possible to use this method to select the order in which folders are placed. If you have a particular folder that you frequently access and begins by the letters Z instead of scrolling down to the lower part of the directory to open it each time, you can label it as the following: 00_FileName. I use this method to list folders in specific projects in chronological order.

It is also possible to add this folder onto the sidebar could be a good idea.

That brings us to the sidebar. I use the sidebar to access folders that I frequently access at the moment in time . There's no reason to save shortcuts to your sidebar when you do not frequent access to the folders. It is generally recommended to have a general folder, such as "Work" in the sidebar and a specific one, like 'FinancialWork-Jan'. After you've completed working on a particular task You can take off your link from this folder's sidebar.

The filename itself doesn't need to be long or complex. In fact the simpler, the better. It's not necessary to include a number of descriptive words for the name of a file - typically, just one word will suffice and you can make use of tags for the filename. If you can, make use of abbreviations, like August instead of August. FinanceReport can be reduced to FinanceRep or FinRep in case that is logical to you. The reduction to just three characters is the good choice. If you are able to shorten the word, and it's comprehendable, go for it. If the word becomes unintelligible by shortening it, then it's best not to.

Filenames that are too long can be difficult to read by you and an operating system. If a filename becomes too long, the file directory will not show the full name,

instead reducing it , and then adding a couple of ellipses at the end.
'

ThisIsAReallyLongFileNameAboutFileNamingConvetions ' would be shortened to something like 'ThisIsAReallyLongFileName...'.

Remember these suggestions and create your own file name convention. Keep in mind that if a third party is able to navigate your directory without difficulty, your naming convention will be successful.

Email

Email is probably the method of communication used the most. Every day, users receive hundreds or even dozens of emails. Because of this, the emails pile up quite quickly. If you don't put in place proper processes in place to handle this, your inbox of emails will soon become chaotic and overflowing. In the present I'd bet you have at least 1000 emails that are not that are in your inbox. What's the reason? They're not needed anymore Why would you want to keep track of them?

I faced a similar issue not too long ago , when I went through my personal email inbox. I had a good 5000 emails, some dating for 10 years! Never thought of eliminating these emails. Instead I would simply mark them as read, then forget about them.

Email doesn't need to be messy, but it does need to be. My inbox is well-organized with less than 50 emails. Some of them don't have to be saved however I'm keeping them for now because I might require this information in the in the near in the near future. However, these emails might be deleted off my mailer.

It's a good idea create an online file, like Google Docs or Evernote, in which you can store important information about your emails. Create separate documents according to the nature of the emails within. For instance, I may keep a file with all my receipts, and another one for discount codes. This isn't the best example as the majority of receipts will become obsolete and discount codes usually do not last for long however, you'll get the picture.

It keeps the relevant information organized it will also save space in your inbox. You may keep a folder that contains all your recent work details This will not only make it easier to go through your email to locate relevant information, it also lets you eliminate many messages from the inbox. In this case you can copy and paste pertinent details, save screenshots or simply write out the most important details in each email. Be sure to include an appropriate date and context to help you understand the details when you return to revisit it later.

Examples of emails that can be deleted immediately:

Old verification codes

Password reset emails

Newsletter emails

Social media / website notification emails

If you're not sure the email hasn't been sent in the last few weeks or the past month, you may delete the email. It's completely safe to do this. If the company or person wanted to be contacted, but you haven't yet responded you're probably not in a position to do so and they'll likely forget. If the message was crucial and urgent, they'd follow up or contact them with a different method of communication.

Where do I start?

The initial procedure of sorting your emails can take quite a long time. I probably spent a about an hour to sort through and eliminate old emails. The only step you need to take is start. Make a block of time to relax listen to some tunes and begin to work. First, you must begin to sort according to date order and listing all of your older mails at the very top. Then, you can quickly go through subject lines to find something that seems important or interesting, then look over the email, and make a decision from there.

If the information contained in the email isn't going to serve any specific purpose within the next few years, remove the message. If the email contains information that you'd like to keep, but won't be useful for a while, put it in the list of documents separately Do the same for sentimental emails.

In Gmail the list of emails that you can view displays 50 emails at one time. You can browse at the subjects of 50 emails, select which you want to keep, and then choose all of them - removing the ones you wish to keep and delete all.

At this point you are able to either start the process of transfer from your email to an external file this means you can erase the email after completion and accelerate the process or save it for later or batch items to improve the chances of Flow. Sometimes, the transfer of information may be ineffective, especially when you are looking at older emails. Transferring information is something that you need to be aware of before you open most recent emails.

Repeat the process. Repeat the process until you've reached the most recent emails, for instance, for the year in question. It's possible that you'll feel a sense of nostalgic feelings during this process and that's a great benefit.

Once you've sorted through all your emails and only kept the most relevant ones, you'll be able to make categories and filters. Filters happen whenever an email arrives such as, for instance I could have a filter that automatically assigns an email to one of a specific category in accordance with a set of parameters. There may be another filter which flags the email as spam, or removes the message. Categories are exactly what they say on the tin. They are categories of emails pertaining to specific subjects.

Filters are especially important to automate the organization of your inbox. For instance, if you receive a lot of emails from your coworker who are not productive It is possible to create an automated filter that will add the emails into the category "coworker A". It is possible to create a filter that blocks email messages sent by your boss. If you frequently receive emails from a newsletter that you enjoy reading and enjoy, you can add a filter that marks the mail as essential and then places it in the category 'newsletter.

However you can mark certain email messages to be marked as spam, or read. Sometimes, I get emails sent by Steam Verification saying someone has attempted to log into my account using an authentication code. Because I am sure that this isn't me - and I don't use Steam and I'm able to create filters to remove those emails. I am confident that my Steam account is safe unless hackers hack my email since they don't have a confirmation email needed to sign into the account. If I should utilize Steam again and require an authentication code to sign in, I could simply switch off the filter for a period of time.

Categories can be useful to keep things organized and organized. If you have the same email address to work and personal motives, categories are especially crucial. Many times, I receive emails from an employer's email address to my personal account, so that I can see everything in a single glance. Here, I've set up a filter that marks forwarded emails from info@thegrowinggraduate.com as 'The Growing Graduate' (my work). You can categorize almost anything . I'm aware that Gmail automatically divides emails into Social, Primary, as well as Updates tabs. To help us organize our lives but, we must categorize into more categories than these defaults.

Many email services permit you to filter your emails using keywords within the subject line. This can be used in your favor. If you frequently receive emails with financial reports that contain 'finance' as your subject, then you might create a category titled "Finance" that automatically categorizes these emails.

While this approach is useful and can help with organization, it's never always 100% accurate. If you're using this category for work purposes when you get an email with the subject "Get your discount on shopping - enhance your financial situation by reducing your debt!' (excuse the bad example) it's likely to be sent to the same location as your work-related files that you don't would like to. Instead, you could create criteria, such as the subject line containing the word "finance" and the sender is via your company's email extension (@companyname.com). This will ensure that you only include financial emails that are related to work within this category. It is possible to add emails manually but don't fret that an important email does not get added to the category.

In the same way, you can also automatically filter your work emails when your company has an extension for customizing like this email sent coming from '@companyname.com will be automatically categorized into a general "Work" category, while emails , such as newsletters, are classified in different categories.

I'm not able tell you exactly the categories and filters you should make, since our lives and email inboxes are very different. Instead, get creative. Consider what emails you receive regularly, and then how you can classify them. It's actually very enjoyable once you're engaged.

Unsubscribing

One of the most important methods to keep your inbox clean and well-organized inbox is to stop subscribing from unwanted emails. Many social media platforms and online websites will automatically send you notice emails that aren't required. To stop receiving these notifications scroll to the end of the email and click "update email preferences" or similar. It will redirect you to the site and display your notifications settings. You can turn off email notifications for anything you don't want to be informed about.

You're likely to be subscribed to numerous useless newsletters. look at the at the bottom of these emails and choose to unsubscribe. It's usually an easy, one or two-step procedure that shouldn't take too long to complete.

Conclusion

The organization process can bring many advantages to your lifestyle and help you to locate the items you need within your home. Instead of wasting hours trying to sort through the piles of items that don't need every day make the effort to arrange your home so that you can see just how easier things can become.

I hope this book has been capable of providing you with some helpful strategies that you can apply in organizing the rooms at home. The first step towards getting organized the way you're looking for is to start by getting up and going!

www.ingramcontent.com/pod-product-compliance
Lightning Source LLC
Chambersburg PA
CBHW050407120526
44590CB00015B/1867